T5-CCV-199

Turk Bird

The High-Flying Life and Times of Eddie Gardner

JAMES H. BRUNS

© 1998, National Postal Museum, Smithsonian Institution. All rights reserved. No part of this work may be reproduced or used in any form or by any means without written permission from the National Postal Museum, Smithsonian Institution, Washington, D.C. 20560.

Printed in the United States of America.

ISBN: 1-891568-03-5

In memory of my father, Franklin R. Bruns, Jr.

CONTENTS

Introduction 1

Chapter One: Home 3

Chapter Two: Sprouting Wings 9

Chapter Three: The Fearless Four 15

Chapter Four: Gardner's First Task 23

Chapter Five: The Race to Chicago 31

Chapter Six: "Have You Ever Taken Gas?" 45

Chapter Seven: "I Laugh When I Read Them Myself" 51

Chapter Eight: "Have Not Accepted the Junk You Referred To" 55

Chapter Nine: The Shy Flier 63

Chapter Ten: Prone to Tales 69

Chapter Eleven: Fly or Be Fired 71

Chapter Twelve: Barnstormer's Mentality 81

Chapter Thirteen: "I Am Still Going Higher" 87

Chapter Fourteen: The Ninth Life 93

Epilogue 99

Photo Credits 103

ACKNOWLEDGMENTS

I am deeply indebted to Christine Zylbert, whose editing brought clarity to my thoughts and sharpness to my words. I would be at a loss were it not for her production assistance and constant care.

I am also grateful to Ione and Norman Mueller of Plainfield, Illinois, for furnishing so much information about the local community and its rich history. Special thanks also goes to Elizabeth Little, my research assistant for much of this book. Thanks also to Milton and Jerry Lipsner for their recollections concerning their father and his early air mail pilots. I deeply appreciate the help of many of my colleagues, including Ruth Richards for her patience in typing the countless revisions to the manuscript, Jack Vaughan for assisting in locating archival photographs, and Dr. John Weimer for reviewing the manuscript. Other assistance was provided by Kevin Allen and Peter von Gomm, both members of the staff of the National Postal Museum. I am also grateful for the expertise provided by Charles Yeager, former editor of the journal of the Bureau Issues Association, and Meg Ausman, historian of the United States Postal Service. I am grateful to the Smithsonian Institution Libraries for providing many of the photographs used in this book.

— J.H.B., September 1998

INTRODUCTION

Forever showing off, Eddie Gardner was a star at the 1921 Nebraska State Fair. No danger daunted him; no feat was too exacting. He had a peculiar adaptability to his chosen profession and he loved to awe the crowds with his aerial prowess: skimming barely inches above the earth, tightly looping-the-loops, and performing other more hair-raising aerobatics. He loved to dazzle the crowd, whose faces often registered fear as much as awe.

At one point during the air show, Gardner's Nebraska Aircraft Corporation plane was struck by sudden gusts while approaching the landing field at the conclusion of his exhibition. The machine overturned within a few feet of the ground. One wing crumpled upon impact, the propeller shattered, and the undercarriage separated from the body of the plane. A swarm of Boy Scouts immediately surrounded the wrecked plane to prevent souvenir hunters from ripping it to pieces. But the boys were no match for the determined spectators, who picked the plane clean like a roast turkey on Thanksgiving Day.

The pilot managed to walk away from the crash, boasting that he was not the least bit hurt. But less than a year later, at another Midwest air show, Gardner would again be pulled from the wreckage of his plane, and this time there would be no boasting. This time the mortally injured pilot would utter one plaintive request: "Please take me home."

CHAPTER ONE

HOME

H ome for Eddie Gardner was Plainfield, Illinois. His family settled there nearly two decades before his birth in 1888. Named and platted in 1834, the village of Plainfield is about 36 miles southwest of Chicago.

Plainfield was a prosperous enough little place. In 1895 a water system was established and the Chicago Telephone Company installed lines. In 1907 gas pipes were laid and power lines were erected in 1909. Despite such progress, the streets nevertheless were unpaved, and they would remain so until about the time of Eddie's death.

Plainfield was indeed a small world. Eddie's early life revolved around the Grange, church, school, and farm chores. For a typical Plainfield farm boy like Eddie, these four pillars set the parameters for determining friendships and family associations, as well as defining one's social place, educational needs, and sense of community.

This confined community would limit the prospects for Eddie's father, mother, and sister — and for Eddie as well, unless he was prepared to break away from it. By about 1910 he would be.

In this relatively closed environment, neighbors typically married among themselves; there wasn't much of an alternative on that score. Eddie's father, Martin, had married a neighbor girl, Mary Augusta Burt, who lived only a few miles from his 131-acre farm.

Both of Eddie's parents were born of first-generation German-Americans: Martin was born in Ohio in May 1857 and Mary in Illinois in February 1859. Martin Gardner and Mary Burt were married in 1878, and two years later had a baby girl, Nellie. Eddie would be born eight years after Nellie.

Following her parents' example, Nellie married a local farm boy, George Spangler. She and George had two children: Pearlie, who was born in 1899 but died in infancy, and Evelyn, who was high

North side of the
Plainfield, Illinois,
business district before
the fire of 1898.

school-aged the year Eddie died. The Spangler homestead, which
Eddie visited often, was typical of the farms around Plainfield.

The Gardner and Spangler clans arrived in Illinois within about a
decade of each other, and each family quickly began acquiring large
tracts of property. Martin Gardner began buying considerable lots in
the 1870s and 1880s, about the time he married.

Eddie was born on the family farm on April 4, 1888. The house,
located on Lockport Road, a few miles west of Plainfield, is still
standing, although it has changed significantly over time. At first the
family could not decide on a name for the boy. His certificate of birth
simply reads " — Gardner." When and why the family specifically
settled on Edward Van Buren Gardner is not clear, but the practice of
naming children in honor of past presidents was extremely common
at the time.

Plainfield had all of the trials and tribulations of small town
America, including its fair share of devastating fires. When Eddie was
ten, the town's center went up in flames. Neighboring farm families
helped the town's 27-member volunteer fire company, founded in
1892, extinguish the blaze, but not before it gutted much of the
business district. The post office was among the buildings destroyed.
In a letter, the daughter of the postmaster, John Sennitt, describes
the fire this way:

> I found Papa and Mr. Beggs shoving things into the
> mailbags as fast as they could. I didn't know what to pick
> up first, so I rushed for the cash drawer. We got the most
> valuable things, like the books, stamps, etc. Then we
> heard people say there were two barrels of gun powder on
> Mr. Hay's cellar liable to go off any minute. When Mr.
> Beggs heard that, he grabbed the mailbags and rushed
> out the back door, for he said afterward that he didn't

want to go off that way. Everyone was afraid to go in the post office from the first on account of the gun powder. Papa still stayed and jerked at the combination boxes, but they were nailed so tight and he had no ax or hammer to work with. By that time the smoke was so thick we could neither see or breathe and great sheets of flame were pouring in through the front door and windows. OH! It was just terrible! The fire roared so awfully on the other side of our wall. I had to scream at Papa to tell him to come out. He just seemed crazed to get those old boxes out and so kept jerking away at them. At last some men went in and got him out. He said he had them apart in the middle and could have gotten them out in five minutes more, but I'm so thankful he didn't stay the other five minutes. It was all so quick and we had no time to think. We had no insurance on the boxes and Papa paid between $350 and $400 for them. On the building, we had $700 insurance and it cost about $1,500 or $1,600, so I can tell you Papa feels blue.

You should have seen our post office when we did up the mail Saturday morn. It was situated in the corner of our bay window on the center table — the remains of the post office. It was a sad sight, I tell you. Before the hack came back from the depot Papa and Grace carried the few books and things to Mr. Beggs' old corner building and there we received the 8 o'clock mail … We have a long line of shoe boxes on the counter, each having a letter of the alphabet and in these we put the papers. Mattie gave us her ribbon boxes for the letters which are arranged alphabetically. Some of the business men brought in shoe boxes with their names on them.

The little, black dusty chair on which you sat while waiting for the mail, the old black stove itself, the office chair on which I whirled, the mail table, the clock, the boxes, and everything else are now a smoldering mass in the ashy ruins.

For the first 11 years of Eddie's life, the Gardners would come to town to pick up their mail at the post office. This ended in 1899 when the town began offering Rural Free Delivery Service. Eventually Eddie would play a major role in changing how mail would be delivered nationwide.

Another presidential namesake, Ulysses Simpson Grant Blakely, one of the Plainfield fire company's founding members, would have a tremendous influence on Eddie. Although Blakely

Eddie's lifelong friend, Ulysses Simpson Grant Blakely.

was 20 years older than the farm boy, he was almost exactly like him in temperament and pluck. That is probably why the two became such good friends despite their age difference. The older man probably could see a great deal of himself in Eddie, and for good reason. Like Eddie, Blakely had little schooling. He loved speed and — in the days before automobiles and airplanes — he used his natural abilities to make money by riding race horses and roller-skating for cash prizes.

As would Eddie, Blakely always relied upon himself. He founded the weekly *Enterprise* the year Eddie was born. His publishing business was a one-man operation. He wrote the news, set the type, ran the presses, and sold the advertising. He did everything for himself and failure was personally unacceptable.

Blakely held Eddie in high regard and that assessment was shared by others too. "We knew his intentions were always the very best," Blakely said of Eddie the year the airman died. The editor knew of the airman's exploits all too well. He was Plainfield's postmaster from 1901 to 1914 and he reported on every newsworthy thing Eddie did. But Blakely perhaps paid him the greatest tribute when he said following his death: "Ed was loyal to his friends." That would have pleased Eddie more than anything else, for his loyalty was a lifelong trait.

Though they may have been alike in character, Eddie and Blakely were different in their background and sense of belonging. Blakely had a hard childhood. Born in Vermont in 1868, he was the thirteenth child in a family of 14. His mother passed away when he was six and his father died six years later. He worked on a farm for a few years before finding a job at age 14 in a woodworking shop in Michigan.

Blakely loved Plainfield. He wanted to be a part of everything the community had to offer. He joined the Masons, Elks, and Lions Club. He served as the president of the Village Board and was the Republican Precinct Committeeman for 20 years. Blakely was glad to have been adopted by Plainfield; Eddie, on the other hand, wanted no part of farming and the small town way of life.

By all accounts, Eddie had a typical childhood. Local historians believe that he attended the one-room Taylor School, which was about a mile from his home. It is known that he was attending school in 1900, but it is not clear how much longer after that he kept on going. His sister's family believes he probably didn't make it past the eighth grade, which would be typical in a farming community. High school was certainly out of the question for all but the brightest children, and even then, girls drastically outnumbered the boys in the upper grades.

If school was out of the question, what was left? Farm life certainly wasn't for Eddie. He found no enjoyment in walking a plow and he hated farm chores. For a young boy whose job was to either pitch or haul the grain from the field to the thresher, bringing in the crops — such as corn, oats, wheat, rye, and barley, which were the staples around Plainfield — was nothing but hard, rotten work.

Eddie wanted off the farm, just like tens of thousands of farm boys his age whose exodus from the farm would become a national trend. By 1910, Eddie had taken up "work" in a pool hall. The 1910 census lists him as "Neither an employer or employee." Instead, he is listed as working on his own accord. It isn't too difficult to imagine what sort of career Eddie was creating for himself. Hustling pool provided an income, yet to a proud farmer like his father, Eddie must have been a great disappointment.

Though Eddie didn't cherish the land, he was beginning to relish the idea of flying over it. This bewildered and infuriated his parents, particularly his father, who considered Eddie's aspirations as a deep personal rejection. The two Gardner men would apparently never reconcile their differences. When Martin Gardner died in 1915, it was with the certain bitter belief that his son was destined for failure.

Eddie's father could not have known that larger forces were at work in American society. Up until the 1870s roughly one-half of the nation's work force were farmers who worked on land they owned. But between 1900 and 1920, the number of farmers fell by nearly 10 percent. Eddie was one of that number. He saw no future in farming. It was routine. It was prone to unpredictable income. It was hard work. And it was simply not for him!

When he left Plainfield around 1910, Eddie had no obligations, no mortgage, no children to raise, and no payroll to meet. He had none of the real-life stresses and strains that were so common among others of his day and age. He only had to live for himself.

His death was in keeping with the way he lived. He would have hated to have died bedridden.

His mother harbored premonitions of Eddie's death, due to a tragic Plainfield accident that remained forever vivid in her mind. Young men of Eddie's generation blew off steam by fishing, boating, picnicking, or frolicking at the Electric Park, developed in 1904 to boost the use of the Aurora, Plainfield, and Joliet electric railway line. Located along the DuPage

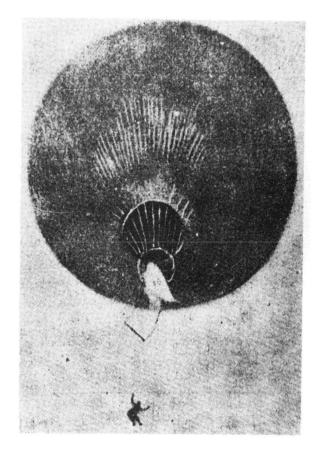

"Professor" Henry Darnell falling to his death.

River at the west edge of Plainfield, the 20-acre chautauqua-like park included a dance pavilion, bowling lanes, race track, and other amusements. A bathhouse and boating facilities dotted the river's edge, and a 3,500-seat auditorium, complete with pipe organ, was a major attraction. Sunday concerts and baseball games were routine fare.

Not typical, however, was the 1911 balloon flight of "Professor" Henry Darnell. The Chicago balloonist was hired to entertain the park's Fourth of July crowd, and he would indeed give them an unforgettable show. While ascending he became entangled in the ropes of his tethered balloon and fell to his death. The incident cast a deep pall over the community — and Eddie's mother — and reminded everyone of the perils of taking to the air. It also provided an opportunity for the town to rally together for a sad but charitable cause. Unable to locate any next of kin, the townsfolk passed the hat to have Darnell buried in the Plainfield Cemetery.

Darnell's death would haunt Eddie's mother when her only son took up flying. There was no consolation in the fact that Eddie was the first Plainfield resident to learn to fly. As far as his mother was concerned, that fact would account for nothing more than a single line in his obituary. She was gripped by a nagging anxiety, an unsettling fear that, like Darnell, her son would plummet to his death in an aerial accident in some distant town, surrounded by strangers. But Mary Gardner was unable to dominate her normally compliant son, and she finally gave up trying to dissuade him. Her fears remained, only to be realized within a decade of Darnell's death.

Nevertheless, Mary Gardner was proud of her son, and for good reason. Few other fliers would have a greater influence on the success of the Air Mail Service in its formative years than Eddie Gardner. She was proudest of the way he "made good" using the skills and abilities that God had given him.

Eddie Gardner had only a minimal education, but he never aimed to be a scholar. He possessed no stunning breadth of vision nor loftiness of ideals. He had none of the "high seriousness" which Aristotle commends to the poet. Instead, his calling was a lark. And his greatest joy was flying among the clouds, pushing himself and his aircraft to do just a little better.

Ultimately, Eddie Gardner was a risk-taker. As a race car driver, flight instructor, and air mail pilot, he possessed an uncanny knack for getting into, and out of, trouble. These were the characteristics he would rely on to build his future, and he capitalized on them exceptionally well.

CHAPTER TWO

SPROUTING WINGS

As long as air mail service could be performed "without expense to the Department," postal officials were eager to give it a try. John Wise's successful balloon flight from St. Louis, Missouri, to Henderson, New York, in 1858 prompted the postmaster of Lafayette, Indiana, to permit the balloonist to carry some mail — at no government expense, mind you — on an experimental flight in 1859. The enterprising postmaster, who wanted to make a name for himself, hoped that Wise could reach either New York City or Philadelphia faster than the usual mail trains.

On August 17, 1859, Wise ascended from Lafayette in his balloon *Jupiter* carrying a mail pouch with 123 letters and 23 circulars. Unfortunately, air currents were unfavorable for a long eastward flight. Unable to maintain sufficient altitude and heading south, Wise touched down near Crawfordsville, Indiana, after a short flight covering about 30 miles. Of the letters carried on this flight, only one is known to have survived, and it is now in the Smithsonian Institution.

Fifty-two years later, Earle L. Ovington was sworn in as the nation's "First Aeroplane Mail Carrier," an unpaid position. He flew mail in conjunction with an aviation meet during the week of September 23-30, 1911, in his 70-horsepower Bleriot monoplane from the exhibition site on Long Island to the post office at Mineola, New York, about six miles away. But Ovington did not deliver the mail in the traditional sense. He simply jettisoned the mail pouch over Mineola, leaving the local postmaster to retrieve the mail and make sure it was properly dispatched. Postal officials considered this type of novel service "quite satisfactory on the whole, and very promising."

Several similar experiments were made during the remainder of 1911, and others were carried out in 1912. At that time, Congress was in no mood to seriously consider funding any kind of airborne mail service. The outbreak of World War I further stalled plans to fly the mail.

Torrey H. Webb, pilot of the New York-to-Philadelphia leg of the first air mail flight, May 15, 1918.

Striking a rather cocky pose before beginning his leg of the Washington-to-New York inaugural air mail flight, George Boyle would not be so pleased with himself by day's end.

By 1918, however, things were looking up. The war in Europe was winding down and with it came a small Congressional appropriation, amounting to $100,000, to enable the postal system to attempt an experimental air mail route.

Because the Post Office Department had no aircraft or fliers of its own, air mail service between New York and Washington, D.C., was begun on May 15, 1918, using Army planes and pilots. One plane was to fly south from New York, while another was to come north from the nation's capital. They were to meet in Philadelphia, where the mail would be relayed on by other pilots.

The New York plane departed from Belmont Park Racetrack, which had been hastily converted to accommodate aerial traffic, bound for Bustleton Field outside Philadelphia, right on schedule. Piloted by Lieutenant Torrey H. Webb, it proceeded the 90 miles to Philadelphia without incident, and the mail was continued on to Washington by Lieutenant James C. Edgerton.

The flight from Washington was more eventful; it was marred from the start by a comedy of errors. Second Lieutenant George Boyle, with about four months' flying experience under his belt, was selected to pilot the northbound mail to Philadelphia. He was chosen as a favor to his future father-in-law, Interstate Commerce Commission Chairman Charles S. McChord. Boyle's selection was only the first of many mistakes to be made in connection with the Washington-to-New York flight.

The Washington-Philadelphia leg, covering a distance of 128 miles, was to be inaugurated before an audience of notables. President and Mrs. Woodrow Wilson, Postmaster General Albert Burleson, other members of the cabinet, and an array of ambassadors motored to a makeshift airfield about a mile southwest of the White House to witness the landmark event. Shortly before Boyle's scheduled takeoff, the ground crew attempted to start his Curtiss "Jenny," but when mechanics spun the propeller, nothing happened. Repeated attempts failed to start the engine. To the amazement — and embarrassment — of the mechanics, they discovered that the plane was out of gas. Workers scurried to drain the tanks of several other aircraft at the field.

Boyle received a hero's send off. His finance, Margaret McChord, was there with an armful of roses for her aerial gladiator. By 10:45 a.m., Boyle's boss, Major Ruben H. Fleet, had strapped a map to the young pilot's right leg, given him last-minute instructions, including the proper compass headings, and wished him good luck. Boyle would need it.

Now with a tankful of gas, the Jenny's prop was again turned and the

engine caught. At last Boyle could go. He eased the throttle forward and ventured off. Once airborne, he was to follow the railroad tracks north to Philadelphia; confused, Boyle headed south. Thoroughly lost, he landed in a plowed field in southern Maryland about 25 miles from his starting point, breaking the propeller in the process. A mail truck was dispatched to recover the mail, which included one letter autographed by President Woodrow Wilson.

Wilson had signed the letter at the request of Noah W. Taussig, who had written to the President on April 22, 1918, promising to have the autographed letter auctioned for the benefit of the American Red Cross or any wartime charity the President preferred. Taussig also promised he would start the bidding at $1,000. True to his word, Taussig opened the bidding at $1,000 when the cover was put up for auction in New York City a month after its brief flight. Taussig's was the only bid.

On May 17, Boyle was given a second chance to complete his air mail run. This time an experienced aviator escorted him in another plane as far north as Baltimore, where the guide pilot veered off and

From left to right, Otto Praeger, Merrit Chance (the postmaster of Washington, D.C.), and Postmaster General Albert Burleson join President Woodrow Wilson at ceremonies honoring the inception of air mail service, May 15, 1918.

returned to Washington. Boyle apparently had been directed, once on his own, to keep the Chesapeake Bay to his right. Dutifully the novice pilot heeded his instructions — and flew almost completely around the bay. Lost again, he landed to get his bearings. When he was certain of his heading, he was off again, and this time in the right direction. However, Boyle was still jinxed. Sometime later the young aviator crashed near the Philadelphia Country Club. Although he was uninjured, his plane suffered a broken wing. The mail was trucked into Philadelphia.

Mindful of the importance of Boyle's future father-in-law, the Post Office Department asked that Boyle be given a third chance to prove himself. Postal officials said that they'd take full responsibility if Boyle flubbed up a third time. Major Fleet, who was the Executive Officer for Flying Training in the United States, with 35 airfields under his command, had no intention of being that forgiving. He repled, "The request is denied. Lieutenant Boyle is relieved of all duty with the Aerial Mail Service and is being sent back to flying school for further training in cross-country flying. If the Post Office Department wishes to place the Aerial Mail Service in proper light before the public, it will take responsibility for Lieutenant Boyle's two previous failures … " George Boyle's air mail days were over.

Between May 15, 1918, and August 10, 1918, the Army completed 251 air mail flights out of 270. Some of those flights included trips to Boston, which began receiving regular service on June 6, 1918.

The general public wasn't sure what to make of the Air Mail Service. Residents along the New York-to-Washington flyway were perhaps the least comfortable with the idea, especially when stories about mail planes crashing into homes began to circulate. The military was partly to blame for the public's fears. In anticipation of the worst, the Army published articles in the popular press, such as the July 1918 issue of *Illustrated World,* with instructions on what to do if a plane did come down. If the pilot and plane came down intact, the public was advised to touch nothing. "The mechanism of the controls is very delicate, and any ignorant, but nevertheless harmful, tampering with them, might subsequently endanger the aviator's life," noted the guidelines. Along with this, local authorities were advised to protect the plane until the nearest military post could send guards. If the plane crashed and the pilot was

H. Paul Culver piloted the first mail from Philadelphia to New York on May 15, 1918. Culver's payload consisted of 350 letters.

hurt, the airman was to receive immediate medical attention, but the plane was to be left alone. "The chief purpose of this is to discover, if possible, the cause for the disaster, so that subsequent accidents from the same cause may be averted." A fourth rule applied specifically to railway workers since the planes typically followed the tracks. They were told to "look out for planes that have fallen so that assistance may be rendered to the aviator to whatever point he wishes to go."

One of the few rebuilt or replica Curtiss JN-4D "Jennies."

As unsettling as the prospect of air mail planes crashing into homes must have been, by the latter part of June 1918, postal officials decided to take over air mail operations from the Army and use its own civilian pilots and planes.

Chapter Three

THE FEARLESS FOUR

I n its leading editorial for July 19, 1918, the *Washington Herald* observed: "The importance attached to the establishment of the [civilian] aeroplane mail service and the confidence felt in its development is shown by the resignation of Captain Benjamin B. Lipsner of a commission in the regular Army to take charge of the operation and maintenance and by the action of the War Department in accepting his resignation for this purpose."

In August 1918, the Post Office Department would completely take over air mail operations from the Army, which had flown the mail for about three months. By that time the Post Office Department had gained a little experience from the Army … perhaps far too little. But ready or not, it would purchase planes of its own, establish its own airfield at College Park, Maryland, and hire four civilian pilots.

Lipsner, who had played an administrative role in the Army's mail flights, sent telegrams to his prime candidates asking them to join his select little flying team. The agreeable

The nation's first civilian air mail pilots flank their leader, Benjamin Lipsner. From left to right: Eddie Gardner, Lipsner, Maurice Newton, Max Miller, and Robert Shank.

pilots met together in Washington, D.C., for the first time on August 2. Lipsner's fearless four were Eddie Gardner, Walter "Max" Miller,

Maurice Newton, and Robert Shank.

Miller, an Army flight instructor from San Diego, California, was the first pilot hired; Shank, who Lipsner described as "a keen and practical pilot, who was punctual, reliable and trustworthy," was the second airman to join the group. Shank recommended Gardner, by then a senior civilian Army flight instructor with over 1,400 hours in the air. Lipsner recognized the name right off.

In March 1918, Eddie, who had signed on with the Army as a civilian flight instructor, was promoted to the position of senior instructor. He held that title until August 5, 1918, when he resigned to join the Air Mail Service. Leaving the Army wasn't hard. He would have to find something else to do sooner or later anyway because the Army was intent on replacing its civilian flight instructors with military personnel as soon as its own teachers could be trained. By December 1918 all the civilian instructors would be gone.

The first civilian air mail pilot hired, Walter "Max" Miller would die flying mail. Miller burned to death over Morristown, New Jersey, on September 1, 1920.

According to an Army report, being a flight instructor was one of the riskiest occupations possible. But as far as Eddie was concerned, training young pilots for the Aviation Section of the Army's Signal Corps wasn't bad duty. The novices were for the most part bright, alert, and anxious to please. The only problem was that they made so many stupid mistakes in the process.

The "flying cadets" attended eight weeks of grueling ground school where they learned navigation, mechanics, and meteorology. Many were discharged for the "inability to qualify as a flying officer" along the way. Morse code class claimed many. For some reason code tests were real killers.

Ground school eliminated about one in four candidates. For those who survived the classwork, pilot training followed. A Curtiss JN-4 Jenny was the typical training plane for cross-country navigation, aerobatics, and formation flying. About one-half of those who made it through ground school would wash out in this phase.

Fatal crashes also took their toll. According to General James H. Doolittle, who was trained in this fashion in 1918, "The basic reason for most crashes in the early days was because the student stalled the plane and got into a spin." Stall and spin recovery techniques were not fully understood back then.

Odd as it may seem, Army flying instructors typically were not much better prepared than their students when they took over instruction from the civilian trainers. They were merely shown a series of moves and told to teach others to do them, recalled Doolittle, who became just such an Army instructor. To be a good instructor you either quickly learned to become exceptionally proficient in the aerial routines or you wound up looking mighty stupid in the eyes of your charges.

Before signing up with the Army as a civilian instructor in 1917, Eddie Gardner was a chauffeur and mechanic in Chicago for several years. During this period he took part in several auto races there and in other cities. In 1911, he purchased a sporty National Motor Vehicle Company racing car from Benjamin Lipsner, who taught him how to drive a high-speed automobile. Like other young men with a little cash and a lot of desire to set speed records, Eddie adored his racy roadster.

Lipsner immediately took a shine to Eddie. Like Lipsner, he had a "take on the world" attitude. Unfortunately, after making the sale, Lipsner lost track of Eddie. It was only after Lipsner began hiring pilots for the Air Mail Service in the summer of 1918 that his name came up again. When Lipsner offered him a job that August, Eddie accepted without reservation.

The job combined a splash of romance and an air of daring ... the perfect cocktail to intoxicate any young man. In many ways, Eddie never really progressed beyond his youth, even though at 30 he was on the verge of middle age. Perhaps in true Peter Pan fashion, he chose not to grow up. He retained the spirit of a chivalrous knight, in the flush of young manhood, searching after some great prize — risking all for the sake of some quest to which his heart clung; in pursuit of some vision seen only by him.

This may well have been a universal characteristic among pilots of that era. Writing in the 1920s, J. Olin Howe observed that "As for romance — those Knights of the air live [their] days packed with it." Air mail pilots were also considered "Uncle Sam's Speed Demons" and their skill and daring would become renowned, so much so that foreign governments soon would pay them their greatest tribute by sending observers to discover precisely how America's efficient U.S.

Eddie Gardner at the College Park, Maryland, airfield.

air mail system worked. This compliment would be echoed in an article published in *Success* magazine, which stated: "So efficient is the service, and so quietly and well is its work done, we hardly realize its existence …" Eddie and his three colleagues laid the foundation for that flattery.

As fate would have it, Eddie was all too happy to join Lipsner's merry troop. At the time, his buddies from the flying school at Dallas were having a real laugh at his expense. It seems that Eddie had earned a few hours of leave and a quick telephone call provided the perfect way to spend it. The girl on the other end of the telephone line was several miles away. Not wanting to waste any time, Eddie borrowed a plane and flew to her house in near record time, rolling up within feet of her front porch. The girl was aghast at Eddie's arrival. She had arranged for the two of them to attend a dance. "Fine, we'll go in the ship," Eddie would recall saying a few years later. "We will not," replied the young lady, "We'll go in my flivver, it's safer."

Eddie gave in and began turning the crank. "Wouldn't you rather go in a baby carriage?" he asked sarcastically. Ever the proper young lady, his date responded, "That's all right, this is fast enough for me." In fact her car would soon prove fast enough for Eddie as well, perhaps too fast. The same daredevil who used to startle his home-town friends of Plainfield with his big National racing car, somehow allowed a rickety Model T to get the better of him. No sooner had Eddie put it in gear than the next thing he knew he was in a farm-house being patched up before being hauled off to a nearby hospital.

Somehow he had driven into a ditch, sustaining numerous fractures, cuts, and bruises; but he wasn't quite sure how or why the accident happened. When he came to, his first reaction was: "Can y' imagine? Me teaching guys to loop-the-loop forwards and backwards thousands of feet in the air letting a tin-Henry put me in the hospital? Never again. Henry can keep his road rabbits. They're too speedy for me." That said, he passed out again.

Eddie was laid up several weeks. Luckily, the girl was unhurt, but her Ford — and their budding romance — were destroyed. Needless to say, the ribbing from his pals back at flight school was relentless. Lipsner's offer couldn't have come at a better time.

According to the hometown Plainfield press, "Gardner was first heard of in the flying game at [Chanute Field in Rantoul, Illinois], where he was hired as an instructor after becoming quite proficient by reason of his natural inquisitiveness … When he was driving a racing automobile, his lines were naturally cast among aviators more or less, but at that time he did not think there was any tangible future to the profession and consequently did not spend much time with it." The war in Europe changed Eddie's mind. He recognized the vital role airplanes could play. "He saw the future of the flying game," said a childhood friend, "and set out to make himself proficient." Actually, Eddie's goal wasn't just to be proficient. He wanted to be far better than that. His sights were set on being extraordinary.

At the time, Lipsner admitted, "Those who know him best are unanimous in stating that he is a modest, unassuming, daredevil … careless, carefree, and happy-go-lucky."

Eddie and Lipsner enjoyed a special relationship. Part of the reason for their closeness was the fact that they were both Midwesterners … and proud of it. But the biggest reason for their bond was that each knew he could count on the other. They remained friends well after they parted professional company.

They shared another trait. They were born leaders. If Eddie had been toiling under wartime conditions in the trenches overseas, instead of in an open cockpit, he would have been the first to lead his troops "over the top," spurring them on, not as a staff officer — which was the kind of leader Lipsner was — but as a tenaciously courageous master sergeant, steadfastly carrying out orders. That was more Eddie's style. The other pilots were attracted to his charismatic, yet informal leadership style. The differences in Lipsner's and

Eddie's administrative styles complemented each other nicely and made for a perfect working relationship. Eddie was like Lipsner's first sergeant.

When he joined the Air Mail Service, Eddie had acquired various nicknames, including "Skeets," "Skin," and "Skinny," which is how he was known to the hometown folks in Plainfield. But, with the Air Mail Service, Eddie

Not a pilot himself, Lipsner was nevertheless photographed in the cockpit of this air mail plane with the appropriate attire.

preferred "Turk Bird." It was a name he was given because of the way his plane would wobble like a turkey as it struggled to become airborne. Eddie liked the name so much, he penned "Turk" on one side of his flying helmet.

The final member of the four fliers was Maurice Newton. At 40, Newton was the old-timer of the group, but he was a steady, dependable pilot. Unfortunately, all of Newton's skill and experience did not help him much when on October 18, 1918, his engine died in route from Philadelphia to New York. What appeared to be a safe landing site, a grassy field beneath him, proved treacherous. His plane struck a concealed ditch, throwing him into the instrument panel and the windshield section.

Although Newton survived the crash, suffering only a broken nose, his family and close friends believed that he never was the same afterward. He stopped flying a short time later and within three years died from what some believe were the results of internal injuries received during the crash.

"His boys," as Lipsner called them, were all former civilian flight instructors with the War Department's Signal Corps aviation schools, each having at least 1,000 flying hours. Their initial salaries were in keeping with those paid to military flight instructors, $3,600 to $4,800. And, as an added incentive, Lipsner arranged for each flier to have a travel commission, which essentially enabled them to go anywhere by train in the United States, free of charge. Lipsner saw this as a way of ensuring that his pilots would be able to get home whenever they weren't flying.

The pay was good, but, as Eddie griped, "This income tax sure knocks my eyes out. It hit me for $180. There ain't much use in working anymore the time you live nowadays." He also complained in letters to his sister that his living expenses were high. "It cost me nearly $100 a month for my room and board." While this was indeed a far cry from the $32 a month he was paying in Chicago a few years before, what he failed to mentioned to his sister was that he was in some pretty fine digs at the luxurious Raleigh Hotel in Washington, D.C.

But was good pay and fancy lodging worth risking your life for? While it was no doubt appreciated, the compensation was not what drew these pilots to their risky work. The sheer exhilaration of flying was probably what lured them. Each week with the Air Mail Service, they could take to the air an average of four days and cover 1,600 miles. It was a dream come true for excitement junkies like Eddie.

Indeed, these early air mail pilots were a daring lot. One later recalled that the group was "considered pretty much a suicide club." The life expectancy of the first mail pilots was as little as 900 hours. But a handful of reckless airmen rose to the challenge. They flew in open cockpits with little more than their nerve and flying skills going for them.

Lipsner had no doubts about Eddie's ability. "For pure bulldog courage and stamina under discouraging conditions, I believe that Eddie Gardner stood head and shoulders above all contemporary pilots, either military or civilian," he would say years later.

While this was an exceptional tribute, Lipsner's words suggest that Eddie never knew when to quit and that he may not have understood — or chose to ignore — his limitations as a pilot. Some may think that Lipsner may have exaggerated the extent of his friend's risk taking, but Eddie's remarkable record of flying speaks for itself. Rather than disregarding his limits, it is more likely that Eddie, like many pilots, simply got too wrapped up in what he was doing minute by minute, day by day, to always fully consider the risks. The willingness to take risks was not always an admirable quality in a flier. Typically, it was a fatal flaw.

CHAPTER FOUR

GARDNER'S FIRST TASK

O n August 5, 1918, Eddie was appointed to a committee
charged with inspecting six planes prepared for the Air Mail
Service by the Standard Aircraft Corporation. The planes
would augment the service's small fleet of war-surplus Jennies and
DeHavillands.

The following day Eddie traveled to the company's Elizabeth,
New Jersey, facility. Also on the committee were Lipsner and James C.
Edgerton, a pilot with the Army Signal Corps who flew the mail
between May 15, and August 10, 1918. Edgerton was now serving as
the chief of flying operations for the Post Office.

Otto Praeger, Lipsner's boss and a man who always insisted on
seeing things for himself, especially if it might generate publicity for
the Air Mail Service, also traveled to Elizabeth. Joining Praeger was
his chief clerk, George L. Conner, and the superintendent of railway
adjustments, J.B. Corridon, from whose division the expenditures for
the service came.

What made this trip so significant wasn't the planes. They really
weren't all that advanced. Instead, this was an important event
because, according to *The Tractor,* the employee publication of the
Standard Aircraft Corporation, "it represented the first commercial
airplane transaction with the United States government."

"Heretofore all planes made were for military purposes, except a
few planes that had been sold for exhibition purposes, but never
before was there a genuine commercial transaction in airplanes,"
observed the in-house bimonthly magazine.

Standard considered this commercial transaction to be another
of its aerial "firsts." It boasted of being the first American company to
build an Italian-designed Caproni and an English Handley-Paige
bomber.

The specifications for the new air mail planes called for a top
speed of 100 miles per hour, a climbing capacity of 6,000 feet in ten

Max Miller received the "first" of the planes from the Standard Aircraft Corporation. His plane was numbered with a "1" and decorated with a mail pouch on each side. None of the other aircraft were decorated in this way.

minutes, and a load carrying capacity of 300 pounds of mail.

The six planes were powered by eight-cylinder Hispano-Suiza engines that were capable of producing 150 horsepower. The typical cruising speed was 94 miles per hour and the flying range was roughly 280 miles. The Standard planes had approximately a 31-foot wingspan, a length of about 26 feet, and a height of roughly 11 feet. Standard hoped that these aircraft would be the first in a large fleet of mail planes, an armada optimistically projected to include 1,000 aircraft.

Standard was not modest when it came to publicizing its accomplishment. In ad after ad the company played up its role in moving the mail. The December 23, 1918, issue of *Aerial Age Weekly* featured a banner advertisement proclaiming, "Storm Does Not Halt the STANDARD Mail Plane!" The number of planes furnished by Standard was somewhat exaggerated in its promotions. The ads used words like "fleet" which evoked images of a somewhat greater number of planes than was actually provided. Such ads boasted, "Day in and day out, regardless of weather conditions, the fleet of postal planes built by the Standard Aircraft Corporation carries the air-mail. Uninterrupted flights have been made through storms that have practically halted all highway travel. On more than one occasion landing fields have been so rain-soaked that the planes had to rise from mud up to their hubs."

While Eddie and the acceptance party were in Elizabeth, a small group of mail service mechanics visited the factory of the Wright-Martin Aircraft Corporation in New Brunswick, New Jersey. The Hispano-Suiza engines were manufactured here, and the mechanics had come to learn how to repair and maintain them.

The Hispano-Suiza engine was the brainchild of Swiss civil engineer Marc Birkigt. He began working on motorcar engines for Hispano-Suiza in Barcelona, Spain, in 1906. The factory later moved to Paris. The car company produced an array of award-winning vehicles prior to World War I. When war broke out, the French military desperately needed an efficient non-rotating, high-speed aviation engine. The rotary engines available at the time were reliable, but they consumed excessive amounts of fuel and oil. These problems were overcome by the Hispano-Suiza engine. It was so superior to any other non-rotating engine that large quantities were ordered by France, Britain, and Italy.

Six different sizes of Hispano-Suiza engines were available by 1918, ranging from 150 to 450 horsepower. The variation in horse-power was obtained by using larger carburetors, expanded induction pipes, and higher compression ratios. The engine was built with eight cylinders arranged in a 90-degree "V" formation.

According to E.H. Sherbondy, author of the *Textbook of Aero Motors,* "This angular setting of the cylinders resulted in absolutely uniform turning effort on the crankshaft, the power impulses being equally spaced from one another, at 90 degrees."

During the war years, the Hispano-Suiza aircraft engine was manufactured by 15 different companies worldwide. The global output amounted to over 50,000 engines.

That August 6, dubbed "Postal Plane Day," the folks at the Standard Aircraft Corporation staged a special roll-out ceremony for their guests. To commemorate the event, the corporation's president, Harry Bowers Mingle, ceremoniously presented wristwatches to Praeger, Lipsner, Conner, and H.L. Hartung, the Post Office Department's representative stationed at Belmont Park, New York.

Identical wristwatches were also given to Shank, Newton, Miller, and Eddie. Jacques Despollier and Sons made the watches using Waltham Company movements.

Mingle also presented miniature U.S. flags to each of the aviators and to Lipsner. Mrs. Lipsner would symbolically present her husband's flag to Miller six days later in conjunction with the start of civilian Air Mail Service from College Park, Maryland.

In remarks during the ceremony, Mingle said he considered it to be a great honor for his corporation to deliver the six planes in near record time. He said that the achievement was due to the fact that all of the company's 5,000 employees, from the lowest office boy to the highest officials, worked shoulder to shoulder in a "real fighting industry."

Praeger responded by observing that "The deliv-ery of these new machines will, we hope, mean the further extension of the aero mail service." He added, "Let us remember that whatever contributes to

Early aviators like Eddie Gardner were instant heroes, especially among children, who would rush outside at the slightest sound of an airplane engine's drone to watch it pass overhead. Eddie no doubt relished the adulation; it affirmed his drive and spurred him on.

improving the mail service, such as the aeroplane has done, has come to stay."

Praeger emphasized that "with the aeroplanes which the Standard Corporation has just constructed, and the planes which the War Department is about to turn over to us [the original aircraft used since May], together with the continued cooperation of the greatest fighting and technical branches of the Government, the Postmaster General is in a position to relieve the Army within a few days of the burden of operating the Air Mail Service."

Following several more speeches, the guests enjoyed a buffet luncheon in the spacious offices of the sprawling Standard factory. At about 2:30 p.m. the group retired to the company's grandstand adjacent to the Elizabeth Flying Field to witness a demonstration flight. At that time, the 5,000 Standard workers were joined by an equal number of spectators. Following a few additional remarks by Mingle, Eddie was invited to take one of the Hispano-Suiza powered Standard aircraft aloft.

Even though he had never piloted a Standard aircraft, Eddie eagerly climbed into the unfamiliar cockpit. He was directed to do some standard maneuvers, but he had other ideas. Rather than fly a cautious routine, Eddie chose to do some barnstorming. He performed a series of spectacular stunts that pleased Praeger, but upset Lipsner, who feared a crash would give the service a black eye before it even got started.

Once back on the ground Eddie knew he was in trouble. Sensing Lipsner's ire, Eddie quickly pledged "no more stunts" while flying the mail. Lipsner severely chastised him later. He told him that while he did want circus fliers, he didn't want to see any circus flying.

If Eddie's antics failed to please Lipsner, they certainly endeared him to the management of Standard Aircraft. They loved the fact that he was willing to show off their plane with such flamboyance. His bravado impressed them so much that a few years later Standard would hire him to demonstrate its planes.

Few airmen would have taken the chances Eddie did with an unfamiliar aircraft. His attitude even astounded his new-found friends among the fearless four, who were only beginning to grasp what kind of flier Eddie really was. "To Eddie, life is one great joke. He cares little for the life of anyone but, if anything, he cares less for his own," Lipsner said in 1920. Eddie would soon be considered the ace among the fliers who took charge of the new Standard planes.

At the conclusion of the August 6 festivities, the fliers took formal possession of the planes. As part of their flights out of Elizabeth the pilots took some mail. Among the mail flown that day were letters from most of the Wilson cabinet and the ambassadors from France, Great Britain, and Italy, plus dozens from other dignitaries. Only one of the four pilots, Newton, reportedly mailed a letter that day. Mingle

had the honor of symbolically mailing the first letter to be flown.

The first of the Standard planes started for Philadelphia at 6:30 p.m. and arrived there about 40 minutes later.

The Standard planes delighted Eddie. They were just his sort of aircraft. Just the right size, he thought. Their speed was fast enough to get him where he wanted to go, yet still gave him time to think about what he was doing. But his love for the Standard aircraft didn't keep him from testing out other planes.

Eddie's goal was to fully master an aircraft once inside its cockpit. He wanted to fly every airplane … at least once. It was almost as if he was possessed by some cowboy urge to break every wild stallion; the greater the challenge or risk, the more he liked it. And, like a horse-

This particular crash involved an Army plane used to test possible air mail service. Between 1918 and 1927 air mail pilots made over 6,000 forced landings. Two-thirds of these downings were caused by poor weather conditions, while many of the rest resulted from mechanical problems.

man, he didn't mind getting thrown. He'd simply saddle up again until he had the aircraft mastered.

Early in March 1919, for example, a new plane was being prepared that was expected to establish a new non-stop record between New York and Chicago. And, as always, Eddie was eager to try out this new craft. "I expect to make Chicago without a stop and if I have gas enough, keep on going to Omaha," he boasted to his sister, Nellie.

Only a few days earlier, Eddie had flown a craft that achieved 170 miles an hour. Initially, he was impressed with the ride. The plane climbed 12,000 feet in ten minutes. "That is over two miles straight up, as fast as a horse can trot a mile," he wrote Nellie. But, on second thought, he wasn't really comfortable with the experience. "The wind was so strong going through the air that it blowed my goggles on my eyes so hard that the rims cut into my skin and if you put your head out it would near break your neck. [I] never had quite such an experience before," he penned.

There were other things he didn't much like about the plane. "This machine lands on the ground at 80 miles an hour. It took me a half-mile to stop her in. She ain't much of a pleasure ship 'cause it was tricky and I was fighting it all the time in the air." Eddie didn't enjoy the struggle. He was willing to simply "let someone else kill himself in it, I don't want it."

Even with Eddie's beloved Standard airplane, crashes were common in those days, including run-ins with chimneys, houses, and trees. One pilot who had slammed into a tree cheekily reported that he delivered his mail to a "branch" post office. Safe landing sites were few and far between, and navigational aids and flight instruments were nearly nonexistent. Some pilots claimed that one of the best navigational aids was a half-filled bottle of whiskey, although the documentation on this is somewhat suspect. Supposedly, the tilt of the brown-colored fluid in the bottle would indicate to the pilots the level of the plane's wings. And of course the alcohol was necessary because ordinary water might freeze at high altitudes. (Never mind that these planes rarely achieved altitudes high enough where icing would be a problem.) No mention is made that the whiskey might also be useful in fortifying a pilot's nerve, which was perhaps his most important provisioning.

To be a pilot in the late 1910s, fearlessness was a requirement because there was no such thing as a truly reliable parachute. There were no well-located emergency landing fields. No beacon lights marked the flyways. No wireless equipment, automatic gyropilots, wing de-icers, or radio guides were available. Even simple compasses couldn't always be trusted. And worst yet, aircraft engines were known more for their fickleness than their dependability.

Fires in flight were common, principally due to ruptured fuel lines or leaky tanks; and there was the ever-present risk of a blaze when attempting a forced landing.

Weather was another problem. Weather tracking at the time was extremely crude, and pilots could never be certain how severe things were up ahead. There was always the hope that what seemed like a threatening storm front would simply melt away within a few miles. But the fact of the matter was that early air mail pilots never really knew what was in store for them.

Initially the Air Mail Service's weather apparatus consisted of a homemade "dispatch board" crafted by Lipsner from a secondhand drafting board. "In addition to weather conditions," Lipsner explained, "this board showed plane and pilot movements, and which planes were in the shop and which [were] ready to fly."

Using simple symbols, Lipsner's four pilots could glean what the general conditions were between College Park, Maryland; Bustleton, Pennsylvania; and Belmont Park, Long Island. Lipsner's meteorological shorthand was "O" for fair weather, "X" for rain, " and "+" for clear skies. There were other symbols for fog, snow, haze, and cloudy conditions.

Lipsner put great faith in his little dispatch board. "I set up a very thorough system for keeping track of daily meteorological condition," he boasted, "and during the next few months [in 1918] we recorded the weather conditions over 20,000 miles of cross-country flying." But the board reflected weather reports from various fields, relayed to Lipsner by telephone or telegraph, and they were not always precise. Nor were they updated as frequently as they should have been. As a result, the information could not be trusted.

Despite all these dangers, Lipsner's four civilian pilots took over air mail operations from the Army on August 12, 1918. The Post Office Department also enlisted two relief pilots: E. Leroy Langley and L.B. Boldenweck.

The mail service's transition from Army hands to civilian fliers came off without a hitch, and for the most part ran smoothly. On Monday, August 12, Miller flew the mail northbound from Washington to Philadelphia, while Shank carried it south from Belmont Park, New York, to Philadelphia. Eddie and Newton waited in the City of Brotherly Love to take it in relay the rest of the way. The nation's capital was Eddie's destination.

To liven things up, Eddie proposed a little contest, first to Newton, who was already with him on the morning of August 12, and then to Shank, when he arrived in Philadelphia. Miller was included in absentia.

Eddie's wagers on anything aeronautical had already become legendary, though the stakes were largely penny ante. That day, he bet his colleagues that he could best Shank's and Miller's flying times. Eddie knew the cards were stacked against him; it was a sucker's bet. He had to fly further than Shank and, although he and

Miller covered the same distance, Miller had the wind at his back. Eddie faced a stiff head wind. As a side bet, he also wagered that Miller, his arch rival, would land at the wrong airfield.

Eddie wound up losing both bets that day, but perhaps it's just as true to say that everyone involved won. For Eddie, these bets were not about bestowing bragging rights. The wagering kept the pilots from dwelling on the hazards of that day's flying. It also was Eddie's way of fostering camaraderie as well as friendly rivalries. His innocuous challenges often kept the mail moving under severely adverse conditions, adding a "do-or-die" spirit to the band. While his wagers may have prompted some pilots to fly unflinchingly into the unknown when common sense would have recommended otherwise, Eddie never wished any harm to come from his bets. Apparently none ever did.

The fearless four's routine traversing of the north-south route along the Atlantic Coast laid the ground work for the Post Office Department's next real challenge — flying the mail to Chicago.

Lipsner's stated plan was to ensure that each existing route was operating flawlessly before establishing a new one. With his pilots' exceptional record of service between New York and Washington, the time was right for expansion. Publicly Lipsner said he was studying where to extend the service next, but in reality, he had already made up his mind. His goal was to connect New York and Chicago, the nation's first and second largest cities, respectively.

CHAPTER FIVE

THE RACE TO CHICAGO

Lipsner decided to expand service to Chicago because of the Windy City's large commercial markets, political importance, and heavy mail volume — and besides, he was a Chicago native. Only after a great deal of difficulty convincing postal officials did he finally get the green light. During late August of 1918, Lipsner brought Eddie and Miller in on the planning of what would be known as the Pathfinding Flights: establishment of an air route to Chicago.

No sooner did he broach the subject with his two top pilots than an argument ensued over which pilot would make the first trip. Each wanted the honor. Words were hotly exchanged.

Friendship and camaraderie were fast flying out the window. "I liked them both, but I realized that while I had the power to settle the affair by denying both the honor of the flight, I didn't have the heart," recalled Lipsner a short time later.

Lipsner's style was to resolve such quarrels over lunch. Things got off to a rocky start at the restaurant, but suddenly Lipsner was struck with a brilliant thought, he'd let both of them go! "Now boys," he remembered saying, "there is no use in quarreling about this. You are both going to make the trip." Instead of having one chance at success, Lipsner realized that he'd have twice the likelihood of reaching Chicago if both pilots flew in competition on the same day. He'd pit his ace pilots against each other. This was a stroke of genius. Lipsner had thrown down the gauntlet, knowing neither pilot could resist taking up the challenge. But it caught the two airmen off guard. Both were prepared to fight for the honor of going first.

Eddie and Miller were momentarily speechless, a sign Lipsner accepted as assent. He hastily handed each a map and explained the most likely route, a direct line from New York to Chicago. From Belmont Park they would fly over Manhattan into New Jersey, across the mountains of Pennsylvania, and stop for refueling at Lock Haven,

Miller, in his Standard plane, receives a mail pouch from the postmaster of New York City.

Pennsylvania, and Cleveland and Bryan in Ohio. Then they would hook around the lower edge of Lake Michigan into Chicago. On paper it looked simple.

The plan was to follow the Woodrow Wilson Airway, a belt eighty miles wide that extended from New York to San Francisco. The unofficial flyway, established be the Aero Club of America in 1917, connected most of America's major northern cities.

Miller and Eddie studied their maps, neither saying a word. Feeling a bit overly confident that he had successfully dodged that bullet, Lipsner continued. Next, he'd have to explain that he'd like Miller to leave for Chicago first, with Eddie to follow a short time later. The mere thought of tagging after Miller would make Eddie choke. "What do you mean, follow?" Lipsner recollected him snarling.

Eddie burst into a tirade. "Do you think I'm a baby? Do you think I have to have a guide to help me set that ship down in Chicago? Wouldn't I look pretty trailing some guy back to where I come from. What would my friends in Chicago say to see me being led home on a string by some guy from California?"

Lipsner quickly revised his plan. He told Eddie he would leave first and Miller would follow. It didn't matter to him one way or the other, Lipsner told them. But it did matter to Miller! "Oh, Max can [follow], can he?" barked the young Californian. "Why, I couldn't follow him a mile without running him down!"

Lipsner finally had enough of their bickering. A simple toss of a coin would determine who went first, he announced. Lipsner flipped a quarter and Miller called "heads." Heads it was, settling the matter once and for all. Embarrassed by their childish behavior, Miller and Eddie apologized and later left the eatery arm-in-arm, making bets about who would land first. The stakes began meagerly — cigars, neckties, and donuts — but soon grew to "millions."

Both pilots were overly cocky. They seemed to have forgotten where they were going to be flying. From the start of Air Mail Service, the ultimate goal was to provide coast-to-coast service, but spanning the continent would have to be accomplished in stages, beginning with the establishment of flights between New York and Chicago. The big question facing postal officials late in 1918 was whether that first leg was even feasible. Between the two cities loomed the hazardous Allegheny Mountains. Pilots dreaded this section of the country, and for good reason. The Allegheny range was a flier's nightmare. Within a few years it would become known as "Hell's Stretch" or the "Aviators' Graveyard." The region claimed more fatal accidents than anywhere else in the country. Plagued by unpredictable changes in weather and frequently fog-shrouded terrain, this stretch afforded few safe landing sites in the event of trouble.

Eddie and Miller thought they could safely cross the stretch and

Miller (second from left) and Eddie (in center wearing goggles) flank the postmaster of New York City before beginning their race to Chicago in September 1918. Eddie Radel, in his flight suit, is second from the right.

gave little thought to the risks. Instead, they saw it as a contest to prove who was the better pilot, and the race to Chicago soon became just another friendly rivalry.

The evening before the race, the fuel pump on Eddie's plane broke, causing the ground crew to work well into the night to fix the craft. Miller's aircraft was in good trim. As an added precaution, ball compasses were installed in both ships.

Just the day before, the two had been bantering back and forth for the press; as usual, Miller got the better of Eddie, whose "Turk Bird" nickname Miller invoked during their verbal duels. "You'll light out in your usual fashion, I suppose, like a turkey," Miller jabbed. "What do you mean, turkey?" growled Eddie. "They call him the 'Turk Bird' on account of the way he starts out just the way a turkey flaps his wings," replied Eddie's fun-loving needler.

But Eddie was fast losing his composure. "I'm kind of peevish and I have always been considered quite a strong fellow … " Eddie barked. Instantly Miller realized that Eddie was seething. If provoked further Miller wasn't certain that Eddie wouldn't resort to violence. Miller temporarily stopped poking fun.

However, as soon as the two were back on friendlier terms — which typically was within a matter of minutes — Miller let fly with another barb. "Look at the checked cap he wears," at which point Eddie exploded with another, far more drastic threat. He said he'd punch Miller if he did not stop making fun of him or his attire.

Miller knew just how to needle the otherwise good-natured Turk Bird. He could plunge him into violent discord with great ease. That was Miller's one great weapon and he plied it with deadly accuracy whenever the mood struck him. Eddie, who was not one for dishing back what he was being doled, was defenseless in these attacks.

The next day Miller was raring to go. Shortly after daybreak, Miller climbed into his ship, revved the engine, and settled back for one of the rides of his life. Eddie was there to see his buddy off. He grabbed Miller's hand as though to wish him well but instead shouted, "Look me up when you get to Chicago, Max!" With this parting shot, Miller took off at 7:08 a.m. on September 5, 1918, in a 150-horsepower Standard airplane.

Nearly an hour after Miller's departure, Eddie's plane was rolled into place. Immediately, it began to rain. Eddie had no luck at all when it came to the weather. Mother Nature constantly vexed him, so much so that he had developed his own contrarian philosophy: "A bad beginning means a good ending," he liked to say.

Eddie, piloting a 400-horsepower Curtiss R-4, taxied off, but didn't get very far. The tail skid was broken. This was all he needed! He was already nearly 90 minutes behind Miller, and unless he could find another plane, his flight might be scrubbed.

Eddie spotted another Curtiss aircraft and, without the least hesitation, ordered the mail transferred into it. He bounded out of his ailing craft and hustled into the other cockpit. The switch took the ground crew by surprise. Like the commander of a naval vessel under violent enemy attack, Eddie began barking out a succession of orders, laced with torrents of foul language. Only one of the mechanics had the nerve to inform the pilot that the plane he was commandeering had never been tested. Eddie, cussing a steady stream, paid no attention. "Is she full of oil and gas?" was all he wanted to know, and "yes" was all he wanted to hear.

The switch also surprised Edward C. Radel, who was accompanying Eddie on the flight, and he lagged behind, wondering perhaps if his pilot shouldn't reconsider. Radel wasn't aboard as a sightseer. He had been sent, along with his toolbox and spare parts for both planes, so that should either plane be forced down, repairs could be made right on the spot.

Radel was not your ordinary greasemonkey. He had been early aviatrix Katherine Stinson's ace mechanic and probably knew planes better than just about anyone. Lipsner hired the Buffalo, New York, man as his chief mechanic at $2,000 a year in the summer of 1918. A complex character, Radel loved music, especially the saxophone and French horn, and later would play with Fred Waring, the renowned big band leader.

As soon as Radel was aboard, Eddie was off. By then it was 8:50 a.m. Not bad thought Eddie, figuring he still might make up the lost time.

Radel wasn't thinking about the race right then. He was racking his brain trying to remember what they had left behind. It wasn't until the plane was out over the Hudson River that he began to inspect the untested craft and realized the fire extinguisher and their lunch were back on the ground in their abandoned plane.

Eddie also started thinking about the condition of the plane. He realized that he was no longer flying in a craft equipped with a new ball compass, and the one on board hadn't been adjusted. He would have to rely on the cheap little compass in his pocket.

The goal was to reach Chicago in about ten hours. Taking longer

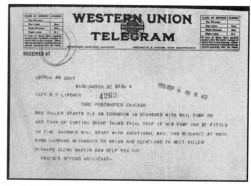

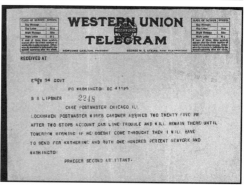

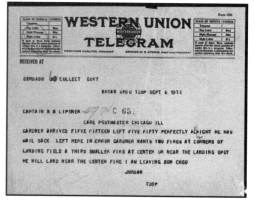

Four of the many telegrams that enabled Lipsner to track the progress of the September Pathfinding Flights made by Miller and Eddie.

would mean either flying at night or making a stopover along the way. Since night flying was tantamount to suicide and an overnight layover would add significantly to the flight, the one-day schedule was a must. If the flight took more than ten hours, the Post Office would do better sending the mail by train.

Once a pilot took off from an airfield, few people knew where he was until he arrived at his destination, if he managed to get there at all. This first Pathfinding Flight was a test not only of the pilots' skills but of the communication network between the air and ground and between anxious postal officials in Washington and Chicago. All along the projected flight path, postal officials advised Lipsner by telephone and telegraph of the progress of the dueling fliers. Lipsner, who had gone to Chicago to be on hand when Eddie and Miller arrived, tried to direct the flights based on these messages.

Eddie made this log report for September 5:

> Had a southwest wind of 18 miles an hour, a clear sky to 1,500 feet altitude, of which was haze and numerous clouds, my compass course to Lock Haven, Pennsylvania, reads 280, allowing for drift was flying 300; but landed me at Wilkes-Barre, Pennsylvania, 30 miles off my course. Landed 11:05, left 12:02, flew this distance at an altitude of 1,500 as the clouds were lower than mountains and had difficulty in finding my landmarks. Weather conditions were getting worse. Hit a rainstorm 20 minutes after leaving Wilkes-Barre, flying at low altitude just clearing mountain tops. Came through out in mountains and landed at Jersey Shore 1:05. Had trouble to start motor on account of water and dirt in gas line. Left Jersey Shore 2:00 landed at Lock Haven 2:16 — a light rain and very low clouds. A hard rain set in, stopped over at Lock Haven until September 6.

The other airfields along the intended route weren't informed of Eddie's decision to layover in Pennsylvania. As the evening progressed, the operations chief at Bryan, Ohio, prepared his field for a possible night landing. He cabled Lipsner: "If night landing is to be made here [we] will have [a] large bonfire [at] each corner of field, with autos lighting [the] fairway, but well out of the field. Land between [the] two easterly fires [and] roll towards [the] westerly fires."

The preparations at Bryan were for naught. Eddie left Lock Haven at 10:45 a.m. the following morning. His log entry for September 6 notes:

> Twenty-mile west wind, clouds lower than mountain tops, flew above clouds at altitude 6,000 feet, just leaving

mountains and located Oil City and Franklin, Pennsylvania, directly on course. To make sure I landed at Sharpville, Ohio, at 12:45, left 1:05, flew for 20 minutes when Lake Erie showed up and Cleveland later. Was delayed 35 minutes flying over Cleveland locating field, landed 3:00 Eastern time. Left Cleveland 2:59 Central time in beautiful weather, only a strong head wind, 26 miles an hour, landed at Bryan, Ohio, 5:15, left 5:50, landed at Westville, Indiana, at 7:20 [p.m.], on account of darkness.

Because of the lateness of Eddie's Ohio departure, the station chief at Bryan, Ohio, sent Lipsner a telegram advising him that "Gardner wants two fires at [the] corners of [the Chicago] landing field [and] a third smaller fire at center or near the landing spot. He will land near the center fire." As requested, the landing fires were set in anticipation of his arrival. But once again Eddie didn't appear.

Lipsner would learn much later of Eddie's decision to put up for the night at Westville. He left the following morning at 7:35 a.m., finally landing at Grant Park in Chicago at 8:17 a.m. on September 7.

Eddie received a warm reception. On hand was Lipsner and an array of postal officials, as well as Charles Dickinson, president of the Aero Club of Illinois, and Augustus Post, secretary of the Aero Club of America.

None of the dignitaries dwelt on the fact that neither pilot had reached Chicago in the proscribed ten hours on the first run. Miller had arrived in the Windy City on September 6, after an overnight layover at Lock Haven, Pennsylvania, and fueling stops at Cleveland

Lipsner receives the mail from Miller upon his arrival in Chicago. Both were disappointed with the results of this first Pathfinding Flight of September 1918.

and Bryan, Ohio.

While Eddie was met with hearty greetings along his way to Chicago, Miller had a run-in with an irate farmer. After he left Lock Haven, the radiator in his plane sprang a leak. In search of water, Miller landed in a field whose owner resented the intrusion. The farmer, armed with a shotgun, didn't give a hoot about Miller's plight and delivered what he said was his final warning before opening fire. Miller scrambled into his plane and flew off in search of friendlier turf. Still needing water for his ailing radiator, he next landed near Jefferson, Ohio, where a more hospitable native offered aid.

Eddie had his share of problems too, including the fact that in his haste to reach Chicago before darkness he had left behind a number of mail sacks in Bryan, Ohio.

By September 6, postal officials in Washington realized that the race to Chicago wasn't much of a showing. Otto Praeger immediately wanted to know what Lipsner planned to do next. Praeger was advised by telegram "Cannot offer any plans until planes arrive here." As far as Lipsner was concerned, the race had been a great test of the aviators and planes, despite its overall lack of success. But he knew he'd have to plan for a return race as soon as arrangements could be made. For now, all he could do was wait for his pilots to arrive.

The race would continue with the return flights from Chicago to New York a few days later, but when the two pilots finally made it to Chicago, they became instant celebrities. They were invited to party after party and went carousing pretty much every night.

Finally, Lipsner had to draw the line. Like an understanding but fed-up father, he reined the pair in and put an end to their late-night outings. "You've got to make the return trip in one day and you must get some sleep," he chastised his fliers. "I hate to spoil your fun but you can't be social lions and successful birds at the same time." It was vintage Lipsner. He, and to some extent his wife Rose, tried to exert a positive influence on the pilots, especially Eddie. The "Captain," an unofficial title left over from Lipsner's Army days, assumed the multiple role of boss, best friend, and patriarch.

Lipsner's use of the term "my boys" in referring to his pilots reflected his strong affinity and concern, especially for Eddie. Lipsner was less concerned about Miller, particularly after he married Daisy Thomas, Lipsner's stenographer. Eddie however was more than just a colleague, co-worker, or underling. As far as the Captain was concerned, his responsibility included watching out for Eddie's personal well-being, like Wendy watching out for Peter Pan.

Lipsner knew Eddie had the makings of a career drifter, moving from job to job, earning a subsistence doing what he liked as long as it got him off the farm. Indeed, Eddie never did the typically grown-up things, like getting a conventional job, settling down, raising a family, and saving money. Whatever transforms adolescents into adults, was latent, suppressed, or absent in Eddie.

The first Pathfinding Flight taught Lipsner that he should not risk everything on one date by sending both pilots out on the return flight together. He would send Miller back to New York on September 9, and Eddie would leave the following day. In that way, he thought, he'd reduce the risk of them both running into bad weather and increase the odds that one of them would make the run in under ten hours.

Miller took off at 6 a.m., on time and in perfect weather. His flight proceeded without a hitch, so well that he chose not to stop at Bryan, Ohio. Instead of landing, he merely dropped the mail sack for Bryan over the side as he passed over the airfield. But Miller's luck ran out around Cleveland, when his radiator once again sprang a leak. Delays in repairing Miller's craft pretty much washed out his chances of sleeping in New York that night.

After a new radiator was installed at Cleveland, Miller continued his flight; but the new radiator didn't hold up any better than the last one. Miller's plane limped into Lock Haven at 7:20 p.m., and the pilot called Lipsner with the bad news. Miller said he was determined to continue the flight even if it meant flying in the dark. Lipsner said no, but Miller insisted he could make it to New York. It wasn't an abiding dedication to the Air Mail Service that drove Miller to complete his run. No, it was something far more basic than that. He had arranged a hot date in New York that evening, and he was hell bent to keep it. But Lipsner made it clear to Miller that he was calling the shots and Miller was going nowhere that night but to bed — alone.

Now it was all up to Eddie. Lipsner fretted. So much could go

Eddie loved playing to a hometown audience. Having grown up in a nearby community and spent several years in Chicago, he was idolized by the residents of the Windy City. Eddie was warmly received by Chicagoans on September 7, 1918, despite being more than a day and a half late in completing his first Pathfinding Flight.

39

wrong. Dawn's arrival would only make him feel worse. The weather was miserable. Mist and low-hanging clouds greeted those gathered at Grant Park to witness Eddie's departure. Within minutes, a driving rainstorm pelted the airfield. The violent downpour prompted many spectators to take cover under the wings of Eddie's plane. This would proved to be only a temporary shelter from the storm.

Eddie was certain the flight would be postponed, so much so that he hadn't bothered to stop for breakfast; but he was wrong. At the appointed time Lipsner gave the word for him to take off. Eddie was reluctant. The rain was coming down in blinding sheets now, the deluge turning the runway into a perfect wetland for waterfowl minute by minute; and besides, Eddie hadn't eaten yet.

Many of the onlookers sided with Eddie. They questioned the advisability of making the flight under the circumstances. They urged that the trip be delayed until the rain stopped. This didn't sit well with Lipsner. He didn't want to argue with his prize pilot and his guests at the same time. "The mail must start on time," he politely told his friends and well-wishers. "We must do our best en route, but we can at least start on time." He also reminded the airman of the slogan of the service: "Uncle Sam's air mail goes on time, rain or shine."

Lipsner had never treated Eddie like this before. He thought his boss was just playacting, so he played along too, which only made matters worse. Unable to get through to Eddie, Lipsner escalated his attack, but the typically good-natured Eddie couldn't believe what was being said was in anger; after all, Lipsner was one of his closest friends.

Thoroughly annoyed by his pilot's attitude, Lipsner ordered the police to clear the field. "I can't shelter you any longer," Eddie said to those huddled under the wings of his plane, "so I'll have to leave you all to the elements."

When all of the guests were out of earshot, Lipsner took Eddie aside and hammered home his point with verbal brutality. "Are you a quitter like a lot of others who call themselves aviators?" he demanded to know. "Do you want the world to remember you as the man who fell down in a pinch?" He tried to ignite Eddie's temper, but Lipsner wasn't as good at it as Miller. "Eddie, you are to land that mail in New York today! Miller has fallen down because of that pesky radiator and it's up to you."

Lipsner played on their friendship as much as Eddie's pride. "Of course if you want to throw me down when so much depends on us both, it's up to you," he remarked. "Do you go or not?"

"Go, of course," replied the browbeaten yet unconvinced flier. "But I haven't had any breakfast!"

"Get your breakfast in Bryan [Ohio]; you should be there in an hour and a half," Lipsner curtly replied.

Finally, the tarpaulin covering the engine hood was pulled back from Eddie's plane and Radel scampered into the forward cockpit. Eddie pitifully climbed into his tiny compartment, gave the command to "turn her over," and the engine was fired up. For a brief moment, Lipsner and the crew strained to hear the engine. "How does she sound to you?" Lipsner asked Eddie as he reached to shake his friend's hand goodbye.

"Great, but … " Eddie replied, looking skyward. Lipsner didn't want any "buts" now! Once again he started in on the pilot, accusing him of being a worthless friend, implying that he was soft, a chicken, a quitter. Eddie tried to defend himself. "I want to be in New York today too," he explained, "and I don't like this start!"

"Neither do I," barked Lipsner with uncharacteristic vehemence. "But you'll be there and I'll look for a call from you this evening the minute you land in Belmont Park."

"All right," Eddie snapped back, his temper finally cresting. "I'll sleep in New York tonight, so help me!"

Gardner wrote at trip's end in his log:

> A steady downpour of rain, clouds, and gloom were all
> that welcomed me in the sky. It was my determination to
> eat supper in New York as I could not be bothered with
> weather conditions, so, at 6:25 a.m., I was New York
> bound.

Lipsner felt horrible about the send off. He had never spoken like that to his friend, but a lot was at stake. He only hoped Eddie understood and would forgive him.

Stepping clear of the craft, Lipsner watched Eddie taxi off, shoot his plane out over the ground, and angle it skyward. In an instant it pierced the grey, low-hanging clouds that blanketed the lake front.

Once Eddie was off, there was again little for Lipsner to do but wait. He was antsy, worse than any expectant father. He monitored the flight from Chicago by phone and wire. Despite the less than ideal beginning, Eddie appeared to be flying as if the Devil was in hot pursuit.

Eddie made it to Cleveland without sustaining any major mechanical problems, but upon landing the anxious pilot discovered that the employee in charge had left the airfield — with the keys to the gasoline and oil tanks in his pocket! This oversight would result in a nearly two-hour delay, a delay that could mean the difference between life and death for Eddie. Had he been able to refuel immediately, he surely would have made New York during daylight. Simple mathematics now told the pilot he would have to fly part of the way in the dark, like it or not.

Eddie's morning log entries on that day record events this way:

Rain and cloud [were so thick] that I would lose sight of [the] ground at 400 feet of altitude. Headed across lower Lake Michigan directly for Gary, Indiana, with a head wind of 22 miles an hour. From there I flew a compass course of 104 degrees, which landed me at Bryan, Ohio, at 8:45. Took on 38 gallons of gas and nine quarts [of] oil. Left Bryan at 9:20. Still raining, heavy haze and fog. Climbed to an altitude of 7,800 feet and flew a direct compass course of 92. After flying for an hour and 30 minutes in sunshine above the storm, I came down to get my bearings and was on the shore of Lake Erie, directly on my course. Landed at Cleveland at 11:16. Had lunch, took on gas and oil. Was delayed one hour and 54 minutes getting filled up with gas. Left Cleveland at 1:12, clouds breaking and clear weather ahead.

Lipsner was advised of the delay in Cleveland. He hastily calculated the flying times and realized the potential danger; his stomach churned in overdrive. He knew Eddie wasn't the best night flier, but he would have to fast become one if the flight was going to end in success that day.

In his log, Eddie recorded the afternoon phase of the flight this way:

Flew a compass course of 104 degrees. Good vision, beautiful trip, and good territory until directly over Oil City, Pennsylvania. From there, flew over mountains at an altitude of 8,000 feet. Flew for two hours and I started looking for Lock Haven. Came directly over course, landed at Lock Haven at 4:47, Eastern time. Took on gas and oil.

Left Lock Haven at 5:45, clear sky, and flew a compass course of 104 degrees over mountain ranges and beautiful levels. Flew two hours, when dark set in. Checking myself on the map, I was directly over Jersey City, straight on my course, with Belmont [Park] not more than 20 minutes on my way.

By dusk Lipsner could only console himself with the adage, "no news is good news." He prayed that Eddie, his best pilot, would somehow come through for him. But the telephone would soon replace no news with bad news. In his book, *The Airmail, Jennies to Jets,* Lipsner recalled the conversation this way:

Suddenly, that evening, the telephone rang. I grabbed it.
"Hello, Captain Lipsner?"
"Yes. Is this Eddie?"

"No, this is the City News Bureau."

"Fine, I suppose my boys arrived O.K."

"No," the voice replied. "I have some bad news for you."

"Bad news! What do you mean? Let's have it!"

"We have just received a flash that Gardner and Radel plunged 7,000 feet from the sky, and both were dangerously, if not fatally, injured. They have been taken to a hospital in Long Island. Their mail plane was completely demolished."

Lipsner frantically tried to locate a plane to take him to New York, but nothing was available. Regular charter flights and passenger service would not become the norm for several decades. Lipsner would have to settle for a train.

Lipsner hoped the media was wrong — after all, they had been incorrect so many times before — but within minutes a telegram arrived confirming that there had been an accident, but giving no other details. He telephoned Belmont Park, but no one there had any information either. All they could say for certain was that the plane had gone down.

Lipsner tossed together his luggage and rushed for the train station. He felt sick recalling his angry words that had perhaps sent Eddie to his death. Was it a premonition of his own death that had made his prized pilot so reluctant to fly that day?

All the way back to New York Lipsner was in a state of mourning. Among the things he thought about was what he was going to say to Eddie's mother and sister. He realized he would have to help make the funeral arrangements. He also fretted over the idea of dealing with the press; thoughts of writing obituaries ran through his mind.

And somehow he'd have to find a new chief mechanic to replace Radel. That wouldn't be easy either.

As Lipsner would admit nearly 40 years later, Eddie "was probably one of the most daring individuals of that time." Replacing a pilot like Eddie would be hard. And Lipsner knew replacing a friend like Eddie would be impossible.

At each stop along the way to New York, Lipsner tried to get further information, but nothing more was available. His sorrow grew more profound as the train neared New York. It had now been nearly 30 hours since the crash was reported, and Lipsner had braced himself to deal with the tragedy. He would still have to present a stern, professional face to the army of reporters he expected to find at the train station in Manhattan when he arrived.

Eddie's trip report for his September 10, 1918, flight from Chicago.

Instead, a much smaller greeting committee awaited him. If Lipsner was shocked by the news of Eddie's "fatal fall," imagine what he felt about his miraculous resurrection. There, waiting for his boss with a sheepish grin was Eddie, a little the worse for wear, but never the less there in the flesh. Miller was there too.

In an instant Lipsner realized that someone was missing. Where was Radel? Visions of the mechanic's mangled body flashed through his mind. Lipsner asked insistently after the mechanic. Finally Eddie set his boss's mind to rest: Radel was in a nearby telephone booth making personal calls. He'd join them in a few minutes.

CHAPTER SIX

"HAVE YOU EVER TAKEN GAS?"

L ipsner was elated to discover not only that his friends had
survived but that their flight had been a stunning success.
"These two were my boys — loyal, able, and true," he would
proclaim a short time after their 1,500-mile race with death.

The Captain wanted to know every detail, but not before the four
had lunch; he was famished.

As the men ordered from their menus, Lipsner learned where
the plane came down and various other fragments, but not the whole
story. Lipsner quickly dismissed the fact that Eddie had crashed
about ten miles short of the Belmont Park airfield, landing instead in
Hicksville, New York. He had instructed Gardner to fly the mail to
New York, and Hicksville was in New York: that was good enough for
him! What mattered most was that the flight marked the first time
mail had been carried between Chicago and New York in less than
ten hours. The actual flying time was nine hours and 18 minutes.
Eddie had beaten the best record of the fastest mail train by well over
ten hours.

As the troop ate, Eddie began telling the story of his flight,
opening with an odd question. "Say, Captain [Lipsner], have you ever
taken gas?" asked the sore pilot. His dining companions were
puzzled. "When I was younger," he explained, "I had to have a tooth
pulled and the dentist gave me gas. I can remember the sensation to
this day." The group wasn't sure what anesthesia had to do with the
story they were about to hear, but they listened intently.

"I was kind of leery of the stuff but after a while I allowed the
attendant to put the muzzle over my face and then they went to it.
They told me to take long, deep breaths, and I did. Louder and
louder went the hammering in my eardrums. I tried to struggle but I
didn't seem to be able to move. I was helpless. Then I drew a blank,
and for what seemed forever I was dead. After a long, long time, I
heard a thin voice calling to me from away off in the nowhere. Then

it came nearer and nearer but I couldn't make it out. I strained my ears to get it and then, with a start, I tried to get up, and I came to finding I was wiping blood off my mouth and that the voice was that of the dentist right beside me. You may think that has no bearing on this yarn but I give you my word, my experience … was much the same except from another cause." Eddie would prove the connection shortly, but for now he continued with his story.

As Eddie told it, for the most part his return flight was unexceptional. He explained that he had no difficulty crossing the Allegheny Mountains, but as he passed into eastern Pennsylvania it began to grow dark. Across New Jersey and over Manhattan, the flight continued without incident.

"I crossed from New Jersey, high above the Statue of Liberty. The metropolis was wonderful. Lights everywhere. Manhattan, the Bronx, Brooklyn, and to the back of us, Staten Island, Queens, and far out on Long Island — lights, lights, lights. They were beautiful, but to me, dangerous."

"It was the most brilliant and dazzling sight I ever hope to see, Eddie continued. "No one who has not been thousands of feet above New York City at night can appreciate it. Neither can they understand the danger. Imagine what would have happened if I had been forced to land at Forty-Second and Broadway or on the Brooklyn Bridge or in one of the rivers. And I was beginning to realize that soon I would have to land somewhere."

By that time Eddie was becoming anxious. He headed the plane towards Belmont Park. When he made it as far as Hicksville, Long Island, he was really starting to panic. With fuel getting low he would soon be forced to land, but he couldn't spot the airfield.

Frantically, he searched the obscured terrain below for the landing flares of the Belmont Park airstrip. For nearly 20 minutes he flew figure-eights trying to spot the field, but to no avail.

Unable to locate the lights that marked his destination, Eddie decided to put down in the first reasonably flat area he could find. "I circled around until I was able to distinguish Brooklyn from New York proper by the inky stretch of the East River between, and I headed out above Long Island in the hope of finding Mineola field."

Air mail mechanic Radel, who accompanied Eddie on his 1918 Pathfinding Flights, was injured when their plane crashed before locating the New York air field.

In the twilight he eyed a promising site, but was unable to tell for sure whether he was looking at a field or a stone quarry.

Gradually Eddie descended. Inching lower, he squinted to make out the contours of the ground. In an instant of panic, he saw what appeared to be treetops — trees that must be at least 30 feet tall he thought! He decided to skim the treetops and then quickly drop successively in two 15-foot swoops onto what he hoped was a level clearing. As he cleared the trees and dropped, the landing gear was ripped away and the fuselage careened along the ground like an uncontrollable surfboard. Seconds later the skidding plane struck something and somersaulted. What Eddie thought were 30-foot-high trees actually were three-foot-tall shrubs.

"My ears were numb from the noise. My eyes were burned out from the flashing exhaust and I felt as if I had taken gas again. I drew another blank, this time what seemed to be the last," Eddie recounted.

Eddie thought it was all over for him. "I was certain this was the finish. On the way down I had sort of expected to get it, but I didn't care so much for myself as I did for Radel. He was strapped in there helpless, depending on me and I had failed him," the flier told his luncheon companions. "I was dead. There was no doubt about it. It wasn't so bad now that I look back on it, as long as I stayed dead. But I might have known I'd have to come back and face the music for what I had done to [Radel]."

Then Eddie remembered hearing faint voices, way off in the distance, just as he had years ago in the dentist's office. He said he strained to hear what was being said, but his foggy brain could not focus on the words. When his mind began to clear, he first remembered feeling something warm trickling down his cheek. He rubbed his face and stared at his moist hand, which he could barely make out in the light of the oncoming headlamps of cars racing to his rescue. It was blood.

"I couldn't help but remember my experience in the dentist's chair. I had taken gas again!" When the dust settled, Eddie — woozy and bleeding — began searching desperately for Radel. He was sure that the mechanic, who had been strapped into the front compartment during the flight, was dead or at least badly hurt. All Eddie could envision was that Radel was buried beneath the engine. Finally, he recognized a faint voice begging: "Take the engine off! TAKE THE ENGINE OFF!" They were the words he had heard only vaguely before losing consciousness.

With the pain from his injuries growing ever more intense, Eddie dragged himself in the direction of Radel's cries. Desperately he tugged at the wreckage, but the twisted hulk wouldn't budge. With the help of bystanders who had rushed to the scene, Radel was finally pulled free. Luckily, he hadn't been crushed by the engine, but had only been pinned under the nearly empty gas tank. Once free, Radel sprang to his feet and began flailing his arms about like a madman. "It isn't broken — my shoulder, it isn't broken — my shoulder, it isn't broken. I know it isn't broken," he ranted.

Radel's antics convinced Eddie that the mechanic had suffered a severe head injury, one that had scrambled his brain. Instead, within seconds a fully composed Radel said, "Gee, Eddie, you're all cut up." Indeed, Eddie had suffered more than Radel. In addition to cuts and bruises and a sprained wrist, the impact had jarred loose the mending cartilage of his nose, which had been broken several days ago in Chicago, and given him a black eye.

But Eddie was suffering from injured pride and exhaustion more than anything else. He and Radel were taken to Vogel's Hotel, in Hicksville, where they were attended by Dr. Otto Hydermann. After some slight patching, the pilot telephoned H.L. Hartung, the air station manager at Belmont Park, and then collapsed. Hartung rushed by car to Hicksville to recover the mail and check on Eddie and Radel, both of whom had by then been transported by ambulance to Nassau Hospital in Mineola. After spending the night at the hospital, Eddie and Radel returned to the airfield to inspect what remained of their plane.

Later, when Eddie told his story to newspaper reporters, he would recall more details of his harrowing flight. "The conditions under which I flew were not ideal. I left Chicago in a blinding rain. After passing over New York Harbor on the evening of the same day, with only the lights in the bay to guide me, I hovered over Belmont Park for 27 minutes in total darkness. There was not a fire or signal of any kind on the black earth beneath to tell me whether I was over the Atlantic, a forest, a town, or a clear field. All the signal fires which were to have guided me to my landing either were not lit or were invisible. Those 27 minutes were the most harrowing in my life. I felt all right myself, but I had the life of my mechanic, Edward C. Radel, to think of. We came down from a height of 5,000 feet to about 1,500, and the lower we got the blacker it became. Finally, I looked down and said we would have to take a chance. I fully expected to run into something and turn turtle." He did exactly that!

After the September 1918 Chicago-to-New York Pathfinding Flights, the Post Office Department switched its refueling site from Lock Haven to Bellefonte, Pennsylvania. Additional test flights were subsequently carried out over the New York-to-Chicago route, but these were marred by delays, mechanical problems, and crashes. But postal officials were undaunted by these setbacks and held out hope of reducing delivery times by as much as 50 percent.

The flight from New York to Bellefonte — and beyond — would soon become routine. In good weather, pilots could navigate simply by sight, flying from one recognizable point to another. On a good day within 25 minutes of taking off at 10 a.m., a plane would cross Long Island, Brooklyn, and Manhattan at the lower end of Central Park on its way to Weehawken and the New Jersey Meadows. Early New Jersey landmarks included a high tower with a red roof, a wooden bridge, and an array of small mills with chimneys belching dark smoke. Ten or 15 minutes later, the pilot would see the Delaware River. Beyond it lay low rolling country and the Delaware Water Gap. Crossing the Blue Ridge, the pilot increased his altitude to 2,500 feet, the safe height for crossing the Allegheny Mountains. Landmarks here included Ring Mountain, with its barren top, and the ribbon-like Susquehanna River. Passing the town of Sunbury, Pennsylvania, the pilot knew he was 180 miles out of New York. Navigating lower over another ridge crest on the right, the aviator would within a few minutes spot a paved state highway — the outer marker for Bellefonte. If the pilot squinted his eyes, Bellefonte's red hangar would be discernible.

After a brief, 25-minute respite in Bellefonte, the pilot proceeded to Cleveland. Here, the plane would be refueled with 60 gallons of gasoline and oiled up for the next leg of the journey, with its own series of physical signposts.

Leaving Bellefonte, the first prominent milestones the pilot would see were the west branch of the Susquehanna River and the Clearfield Mountains. The safe altitude for the mountain crossing was 3,000 feet. At that height the tracks of the Pennsylvania Railroad would be plainly visible amid the flat patchwork of farms. In the far distance, Lake Erie would come into view, proclaiming that the aircraft was approaching Cleveland. The descent into Glenn Martin Field, with its cinder runway, would be long and gradual.

After Cleveland, the terrain would become somewhat monotonous: an endless panorama of towns and villages, punctuated by the lake shore, which gradually veered away from view. Below, the steel mills of Lorain marked another milestone on the way to Chicago.

Bryan, Ohio, was the next stopover. After that, the pilot would head into northern Indiana, passing LaPorte and South Bend off to the right. Soon the smoke and haze from Gary, Indiana, would become visible. South Chicago, with more telltale smoke, rose in the distance.

Maywood Field lay west of Chicago. With its white-bordered cinder runway, it was considered one of the finest mail fields in the country. Planes could land from almost any direction and in almost any weather.

These flyway features would be firmly fixed in the minds of pilots like Eddie Gardner who dared to bridge the gap between New York and Chicago. Under ideal circumstances, visual signposts were exceptionally helpful navigation points. Unfortunately, air mail pilots seldom flew under ideal conditions.

CHAPTER SEVEN

"I LAUGH WHEN I READ
THEM MYSELF"

With the dawning of the age of flight, the public devoured every daring account of an aviator's success … or failure. They marvelled at the pilot's ability to take whatever nature and chance dished out and still succeed.

Eddie also marvelled at his exploits and kept mementoes of his adventures. Like other air mail pilots of his day, he had a scrapbook. "I have most of all my pictures and newspaper clippings from my different trips. It makes quite a [scrapbook], but I hardly ever see it as someone else has always got it, but it's a funny book, [with] a lot of funny write-ups [especially] my smash [on September 10, 1918]. I laugh when I read them myself," he told his sister.

The press was forever exaggerating Eddie's trials and tribulations, and their coverage of his September 10 crash especially irked him. According to one newspaper, "The engine of the airplane carrying Gardner and Edward Raddle (sic), the mechanician, 'went dead' when they were at a height of seven thousand feet, but the pilot did not lose control of the machine and volplaned most of the distance to the ground."

This was pure bunk! To Eddie, such obvious fabrications could not go unchallenged and he rushed to defend his favored Liberty engine. "The story of my 'fall' is not true," he informed the press. "The Liberty motor is the best machine so far made for cross-country flying. It is most dependable and attacks on it are unfair … If it hadn't been that I tried to land in the dark, I would not have lost my landing gear and been shaken up," he explained.

Other aviators agreed with Eddie's defense. Lipsner called the Liberty engine "a wonderful piece of mechanism and the best engine ever placed in an airplane." The 12-cylinder Liberty had been used in mail planes since roughly the start of the service, without giving the least bit of trouble.

The press also misreported the time of the Chicago-to-New York crash, which occurred at 8:20 p.m. According to various newspapers, the wreck took place at 10:50 p.m., 11 p.m., and 1 a.m., all times when the aircraft would have long since run out of gas.

But like all publicity hounds, Eddie never really hated the news media. In fact, he used newspaper reporters to help promote the mail service and serve his own ends. He was no bureaucrat, and he had little faith in paper shufflers; but, he knew that when articles about his exploits appeared in the press, often some sort of favorable administrative action would occur. Eddie used the publicity generated by his September crash to press for various safety improvements, including the installation of electric landing lights. "As soon as arrangements are made to have electric lighting installed at Belmont Park, flying at night will be fairly easy and it will be possible to start out or land before daylight or after dark, without any trouble," he told reporters shortly after his crash.

The day after his Chicago-to-New York flight, Eddie set his sights on another challenge — flying to Europe. "I don't know just when I shall start, but I am ready," he told reporters on September 11, 1918. But, to accomplish this, he'd need a powerful plane and an extraordinary plan. Unknown to reporters, Eddie was once again using them to his — and his boss's — end. Lipsner wanted his boys to make a run at the Atlantic crossing, and Eddie was serving as his mouthpiece.

Eddie was willing to risk such a trip in a regular Liberty-powered plane. He envisioned making eight to ten stops along the way, landing on the decks of transport ships posted at sea at specific intervals for oil, gasoline, food, and rest breaks for himself and a mechanic. With a Liberty-powered plane, he expected the trip across the Atlantic would take about four days. But a better plane was being built that would make the flight much easier, and Lipsner had his eyes on it.

During World War I, the Navy wanted to develop a way of transporting large amounts of supplies across the Atlantic other than by ship. This was crucial, naval planners thought, because the German U-boat threat made ship crossings uncertain and costly. Big seaplanes appeared to be the answer, but by the time such experimental "flying boats" could be built, the war was nearing a close. Still, it was decided to build four such planes and attempt to fly them to Europe. They were designated the NC-1, NC-2, NC-3, and NC-4; the "N" standing for "Navy," and the "C" for "Curtiss," the maker of the crafts.

The four planes were gigantic. Their wing span measured 128 feet and their length was 65 feet. They were powered by 400-horsepower Liberty engines.

Lipsner and his mail pilots realized that here were four naval planes — apparently readily available — that could each carry four and a half tons of mail across the Atlantic. All they needed was one of the planes to prove the feasibility of the flight. If the Navy would turn over the NC-1, being constructed by Glenn Curtiss at Garden City, Long Island, Eddie was certain that he and Miller could make the flight.

Eddie knew they were on the right track when he heard the results of an NC-1 test flight. Piloted by Lieutenant David H. McCullough, the seaplane left the Naval Air Station in Rockaway, Long Island, on November 27, 1918, on a shakedown flight carrying 50 men. That was an unheard-of cargo capacity. Unfortunately, immediately after this flight, the big seaplane was all but forgotten ... but not by Eddie and Lipsner.

In January 1919, Lipsner produced a small promotional pamphlet at his own expense that highlighted the promise of commercial aviation. He sent copies to each member of Congress as well as leaders in the aviation world. The pamphlet pointed out that the NC-1 represented America's best chance to maintain its aeronautical superiority.

In February 1919, Lipsner went so far as to publicly bet Alan Hawley, the president of the Aero Club of America, $10,000 that Eddie and Miller could cross the Atlantic in the NC-1 if given the opportunity. And they would do it within 30 days!

The newspapers made a great deal over the wager, but Hawley was powerless to accept. The NC-1 belonged to the Navy, and Secretary of the Navy Josephus Daniels wasn't willing to turn the flying boat over to Lipsner, or anyone else. Daniels had his sights set on a naval triumph.

When the NC-2 was damaged early in 1919, it was cannibalized for spare parts for the other three planes. On May 8, 1919, the three remaining ships set out for Europe. They were first flown from Rockaway to Halifax, Canada, and from there to Trepassey, Newfoundland. On May 16, the small squadron left Trepassey, bound for the Azores. No sooner were they aloft than bad weather set in. Much

The only "flying boat" to finish its trans-Atlantic demonstration flight, the NC-4 safely landed at Lisbon, Portugal, on May 27, 1919. The NC-1 and the NC-3 were forced down before reaching the Azores. The NC-2 never flew in the demonstration flights.

of that night rain splashed about the wings and flowed into the open cockpits; the wind tugged frantically at the tiny windshields. By dawn on May 17 the fliers plowed on, high above clouds piled high like jutting mountain peaks.

Both the NC-1 and NC-3 were forced down some 100 miles from the Azores. Both were damaged and unable to continue. But the NC-4 flew on, safely arriving in the Azores on May 20. From there the sole surviving plane flew to Lisbon, Portugal, arriving on May 27. It reached its final destination, Plymouth, England, on May 31. Eddie was crestfallen that he hadn't participated in the flight. However, his disappointment might have been lessened had he known that the NC-4 did indeed carry mail, albeit just one piece.

While in Halifax, Navy machinist Pat Carroll had written a letter to his brother, Charles, a corporal with the American Expeditionary Forces stationed in France. Carroll asked another machinist, Eugene "Smokey" Rhodes, to take the letter with him and mail it after the flight. Rhodes had been assigned to the crew of the NC-4 at the last minute because the plane's chief mechanic, E.H. Howard, had been injured by a propeller. Rhodes did not forget Carroll's four-page letter; he mailed it from Lisbon. That piece of mail, the first NC-4 cover, is now in the Smithsonian Institution's National Postal Museum. The NC-4 itself has been restored and is on display at the Smithsonian's National Air and Space Museum.

Chapter Eight

"HAVE NOT ACCEPTED THE JUNK YOU REFERRED TO"

Buoyed by the success of the September Pathfinding Flights, Lipsner announced that the Post Office Department would start regular service between New York and Chicago on October 1, 1918. But his pronouncement was far too premature.

While the September flights showed that New York-Chicago service was possible, establishing the route on a permanent basis proved harder to accomplish. The onset of winter made the connecting service iffy at best with the equipment then on hand. And expanding service to Chicago would also require additional pilots. Lipsner quickly hired ten pilots, in addition to the four emergency fliers and four regular pilots he already had flying on the Washington-to-New York route.

Additional airplanes also were required, for which Lipsner turned to his former Army buddies. Lipsner was never one to look a gift horse in the mouth, so when six surplus military aircraft were offered, he jumped at the opportunity.

Elated by this stroke of luck, Lipsner, Eddie, and several other airmen traveled by train to Houston, Texas, to pick up the six planes the War Department had graciously offered for the new Chicago route. Their optimism quickly soured, however, when they arrived at the Houston base. Although the secondhand planes looked gorgeous on the outside, with a fresh coat of dope applied over the tough, fabric-wrapped wings, mechanically the shiny crafts were absolute trash, in most cases unable to even get off the ground. The planes' engines were nearly impossible to start, and once they did turn over, it seemed as if they were tied to the ground. The engines tended to cut off before the ships could become airborne, and one that did take flight wound up in a tree a short distance from the runway. Eddie finally gave up trying to coax his machine into the air, complaining, "I thought I could fly anything — but not this!"

The troop of fliers went back to their hotel, frustrated and angry. Somehow, news of their tribulations had traveled fast, so fast that a telegram from Otto Praeger was waiting for Lipsner when he arrived at the hotel. The telegram read: "Congratulations on the junk your Army buddies handed you."

Lipsner didn't appreciate Praeger's slap. He cabled Praeger back: "Congratulations not in order. Have not accepted the junk you referred to."

Without viable planes, Lipsner had to postpone the October 1918 inaugural of the Chicago-to-New York service. But Lipsner was reluctant to blame the Army and its useless planes for the delay. Instead, he claimed the delay was due to an "inability to obtain labor and difficulty in acquiring landing places." The start date for the east-to-midwest service would be postponed over and over again, and continuous service between New York and Chicago would not be fully established until the following July.

Praeger's telegram had added insult to an already ailing Lipsner. He had come down with "Spanish Influenza" while in Texas and was a mighty sick man. He was so ill that upon returning to Chicago he immediately checked into the Michael Reese Hospital.

Three of the airmen on that trip had also contracted the flu and were unable to fly, which was okay with Eddie. Instead of remaining in Chicago with his ailing comrades, he rushed back to Washington. He didn't mind filling in for them while they recuperated, since it meant more flying hours for him.

In fact, Eddie was nursing a slight case of influenza himself. "I guess I have the regular flu cause god I never had a cold like this one, so I call it the flu anyway," he told his sister. He didn't want to be pampered, nor did he care much for doctors. Anyway, he knew exactly how to treat his illness: eat onions and drink whiskey.

It was lucky for him that Lipsner was so sick and unaware of Eddie's self-medication. Temperance was a commandment in Lipsner's organization. He would sack a flier over insobriety, as pilot W. Knox Martin found out. His August 20, 1918, letter to Lipsner says it all:

> On the night of August 15th, while in Washington, D.C., I, W. Knox Martin, at that time in the employ of the U.S. Aerial Mail Service as aviator pilot, was intoxicated. This state of intoxication was not a planned or premeditated affair.
>
> Being a man who does not indulge much in alcoholics, the comparatively small amount I did take went to my head.

Eddie, seated on the engine cowling, loved to fly and would take any opportunity to add to his time aloft. When his colleagues came down with the flu in 1918, he happily filled in for as many of them as possible.

I do not make this statement to try to excuse myself from the fact that I did drink when I should not have done so. For the offense I wish to say that I am honestly and heartily sorry.

On August 18th, I was dismissed from the U.S. Aerial Mail Service.

The purpose of this letter is to ask that I be reinstated in the Aerial Mail Service, with the sincere promise that I shall never be guilty of a repetition of the above named offense.

As a profusion of words are unnecessary, and only facts are essential in a case of this sort, and as I believe that I have made myself clear, I will close by asking that this, my letter, be given consideration and that the penalty of absolute dismissal be reconsidered and that I be given another chance to prove my real worth to the United States Aerial Mail Service.

How much of this was actually Martin's thoughts is unclear. His letter for forgiveness was apparently written at the Raleigh Hotel in Washington, D.C., on hotel stationery, possibly penned in Eddie's room, and more than likely developed with Eddie's input. But it didn't work. Lipsner wouldn't take Martin back.

Lipsner's refusal to reinstate Martin was odd, given that he knew his pilots drank, most to excess. Martin appears to have been fired as a warning to the others. By making an example of Martin, Lipsner apparently hoped to impress upon the other fliers that the sin of insobriety was not some heretic rule that could simply be ignored. But the message did not take. Alcoholism was a common affliction among the air mail men. If Lipsner really intended to get tough, he would pretty much have had to fire all his airmen.

"They were all boozers, big beer drinkers, back then," Lipsner's son Jerry would affirm much later.

The order to stay sober was one of many policies and procedures that rankled the pilots, including Eddie. As an air mail pilot, Eddie's work was dictated by timetables; departures and arrivals were highly regimented. But, in contrast, his personal life had no itineraries. Nearly everything that he did outside of work was improvisation. Unplanned happenstance was more to his liking than thoughtful planning and design; Eddie was be no means unique among pilots in this respect.

But Lipsner's rules reflected his concern for his pilots' safety as well as the reliable delivery of the mail. Frequently a pilot's best navigational instruments were his own senses. When flying over unfamiliar terrain, a compass was handy but not always reliable, for under certain circumstances the needle would merely wobble aimlessly. Instead, pilots tended to fly more by dead reckoning, and anything that might muddle their vision could doom the mission. Flying from point to point, pilots would watch for landmarks along the way. And following train tracks — "the iron compass" — was always a good way to navigate, provided you were following them in the right direction, unlike the hapless George Boyle.

A regulation prohibiting air mail pilots from wearing spurs while flying was apparently prompted by the occasional damage to the aircraft. But many of the pilots seemed to believe that "rules were meant to be broken" and took delight in getting away with small, rebellious acts.

Lipsner himself occasionally bent, if not broke, the rules. Miffed that his boss Praeger had decided not to use Handley-Paige bombers for cross-country flying, Lipsner tried to manipulate the press in his favor with a Thanksgiving Day feast aboard one of the massive planes.

The November 28, 1918, "banquet in the clouds" was intended to persuade the postal service to use Handley-Paige bombers, which Lipsner believed could successfully carry a ton and a half of mail at a speed of roughly 100 miles per hour. During the "Thanksgiving Dinner in the Air," he and eight others feasted on turkey and fixin's for 22 minutes in the cabin of one of the giant bombers as it soared 2,500 feet above Elizabeth, New Jersey. The stunt received a great

deal of favorable press but failed to impress postal officials.

The Handley-Paige bombers were available because by late 1918 the war in Europe was winding down. Congress was searching for ways to make the most of the vast amount of surplus equipment on hand, and a rider to the Post Office's appropriation bill enabled the mail system to inherit an armada of spare planes, as well as a legion of Army-trained aviators, plus 170 new aircraft engines. One provision of the rider called for the Secretary of War to turn over more than 200 planes, including 100 DeHavillands and an equal number of lumbering Handley-Paige bombers. Ten Glenn Martin day bombers also were to be given to the Air Mail Service.

This allotment represented far more planes than the postal service could handle, but in December 1918 a reasonable number were accepted. The Handley-Paige, with its 400-horsepower Liberty engines and massive payload capacity, was exactly the ship Lipsner wanted for the New York-to-Chicago run. And he wanted Eddie to be one of his ace bomber jockeys on the route.

But Praeger pulled rank again, flatly killing the use of the Handley-Paige as a frontline mail plane. He spelled out his plans in a December 3, 1918, letter to Lipsner. The Handley-Paige bomber would be used only as backup aircraft in the event of severe emergencies. Instead, Praeger approved use of a small number of Curtiss R-4s, which had a slower landing speed and greater chance of surviving in the event of a forced landing over the risky terrain between Eliza-

As a promotional gimmick, Lipsner and several others dined in a Handley-Paige bomber on Thanksgiving Day, 1918, to demonstrate the craft's enormous capacity. Postal officials were unimpressed by the picnic feast and Lipsner's attempts to manipulate them through the press.

beth, New Jersey, (which by then had replaced Belmont Park, New York, as the eastern end of the New York-Washington route), and Bellefonte, Pennsylvania, which was planned as a convenient relay point and refueling stop.

According to Praeger's plans, the DeHavillands would be used between Bellefonte and Chicago. In this way, Praeger said, "we do not have to carry Curtiss R-4 parts and equipment at each field between New York and Chicago." His reasoning made perfect sense, and it allowed him to rein Lipsner back in line. "As you know," he told Lipsner, "this leaves out for the time being operation of the Handley-Paiges."

Lipsner was outraged. Praeger was making all the crucial decisions about the Air Mail Service, leaving Lipsner no opportunity to be heard. Again Lipsner turned to the media to sway public opinion. But this time Lipsner was too bitter and said too much. He had no choice but to resign.

Lipsner told reporters "I refuse to be a part in anything that is not being conducted aboveboard." He intimated that Praeger may have struck a deal with airplane manufacturers. "Can it be right to throw away millions of dollars' worth of serviceable Army airplane equipment so that the airplane factories which now have been forced to close down can reopen and continue making huge profits?" he asked. He said that he could operate the system his way with the Handley-Paiges, if given a chance. "This, I am sure can be done with the aeroplane being turned over to the Post Office Department by the War Department without any extensive expenditure of the public's money," Lipsner insisted.

To help prove his point he had Miller fly one of the big planes after only ten minutes of training. Miller successfully flew the giant plane alone and made a perfect landing.

Lipsner was mad enough to go after Praeger and Postmaster General Albert Burleson with all the vehemence he could muster. He launched into a vicious media campaign aimed at embarrassing his former chiefs.

Lipsner's resignation and his attacks on the postal officials appeared in dozens of newspapers nationwide, but they had little effect. Praeger and Burleson were too well insulated to suffer any real damage from a political flyweight like Lipsner.

Indeed, Burleson had survived much worse. In 1916 a member of the Senate launched an investigation into Burleson's use of convicts to farm his property in Texas a few years earlier. The Burleson and Johns Farm, a splendid tract of 5,000 acres bordering on Hill and Bosque counties, was cultivated by approximately 80 state convicts who were allegedly beaten, tortured, and killed for the slightest infraction. Burleson and the state shared in the proceeds from the convict-labor cotton farm, with 60 percent going to Texas and 40 percent to Burleson and a relative.

According to the senator who had begun the inquiry, "Out of such labor, out of such profits from a state convict, out of such a tainted source, Postmaster General Burleson has become the wealthiest member of the Democratic cabinet today." The senator said that he wasn't sure if the information was known at the time of Burleson's appointment to head up the postal system; but "it will not be unknown from now afterwards."

Perhaps the worst charge of political cronyism to come out of the Burleson investigation was the alleged preference given to Thomas Durham. The one-time state foreman at the farm, Durham was indicted for the death of one of the convicts. Tried in 1911, Durham was subsequently acquitted because the state could produce nothing but the eyewitness testimony of African-American convicts, which was summarily discounted. Two years after Durham's acquittal, Burleson was said to have been instrumental in Durham's appointment as postmaster of Longview, Texas. According to the senator leveling the charges, this action outraged the congressman from that district, as well as many of the leading families from the community. But Burleson had his way, and Durham remained as postmaster until his death a year later.

Burleson did not appreciate the senator's assertions, labeling all the charges "vilely false." Burleson pointed out that he was part owner of a plantation which the state itself leased and operated and that the foreman, the plantation superintendent employed by the state, was acquitted of a murder charge that had been made solely for political purposes. And Burleson contended that Durham's appointment as postmaster was made with the acquiescence of the congressman from his district.

Burleson and Praeger stood by their friends and scorned their enemies, and Lipsner was now in the latter camp.

CHAPTER NINE

THE SHY FLIER

Having Chicago as his terminus was ideal for Eddie. It meant that he could see his mother, sister, and hometown buddies more often. He figured he could jaunt down to Plainfield by claiming that he had to check out the airworthiness of his plane between mail runs. And once home, he was sure to be the star attraction.

Eddie's plans worked out perfectly. It seemed that every time he was in Chicago, he was asked to test out some new plane. Since a typical trial might involve at least a two-hour test flight, nobody would mind if he buzzed into Plainfield. He told his sister, "The old Grange hall may lose its chimney 'cause I could fly down (to Plainfield) in 20 or 25 minutes from the field and make a good test."

Eddie relished the idea of seeing his family more often. He sorely missed them, especially his sister's kids. He doted on them. The only problem was making the New York-to-Chicago flights in the winter. "I would like to come back west but as to flying all winter there, I am studying whether to come back or stay here. I would like to be back home, but if I thought I would have to fly next winter I think I would stay here, but I hope to be off the route by then," he told his family.

And the folks back in Plainfield doted on their famous flyboy, and the local newspaper printed great prose about its native son. This account, published in late fall of 1918, exaggerates some facts but reveals something of the flying conditions of the time:

> Milton R. Wood was returned from a trip to Connecticut, New York City and Washington, where he spent the holidays, and reports meeting [one] of our Plainfield boys that [has made] good records for [himself] and our town. By special permit he visited the landing grounds and roosts where the big birds rest after Ed rides them be-tween Washington and New York every day, making trips

of nearly 300 miles in two hours, he saw Ed landing in the
field where last week's rains had made small lakes and
mud holes, but Friday night's freeze had covered with ice,
too thin to carry a 2,000 [pound] bird on skates and too
thick to swim but it did not seem to worry Ed a little bit
for he turned on [the] power and it was hard to tell
whether he was flying or swimming for about half a mile
but she soon reached port.

Eddie was deeply honored by the adoration of the Plainfield
community, especially its children. He sought to thank them with
worthy deeds and thoughtful acts. During a visit home in August
1918, he added some excitement to an annual picnic sponsored by
the Plainfield Grain Company by buzzing the grounds and staging an
impromptu stunt show. Everyone knew the daring airman had to be
"their Eddie." And Eddie made sure the hometown folk — especially
the young girls — knew they would always be welcome to joyride in
his plane.

Despite his acts of showmanship, Eddie was shyer than most
people realized. Although he was often in the spotlight and could
easily speak to crowds, he was more taciturn when with just one or
two people. Occasionally Eddie's silence in small groups would make
for awkward moments. But it was no reflection of his regard for his
company, only his shyness.

Eddie's hometown neighbors remember him as naturally shy,
never one to "push himself forward." But his reticence probably cost
him a great deal of celebrity. Because he had a better way with words,
Miller generally got more press. For every column inch of press
coverage Eddie received, the outgoing and gregarious Miller got six.

Eddie wasn't shy however when it came to his clothing. He always
dressed the part, typically clad in the rakish togs favored by early air
mail pilots. In winter he wore a top-of-the-line one-piece flying suit
like those worn by Army aviators. Along with this $65 winter outfit he
wore an expensive leather aviator's hood. This soft leather head gear,
which was considered particularly windproof, was identical in pattern
to those worn by European aviators in cold weather. A face mask,
ribbed wool socks, warm gloves, and non-splinterable safety goggles
completed the winter outfit. When not in the air, or for summer
flying, his costume included a flashy leather flying jacket, leather
puttees, and Army-style flying trousers.

Officially, Eddie and his flying buddies were designated as
"aviator pilots." Some in the group considered the title sufficient,
believing that sometimes too much title and uniform is a handicap.
But Eddie disagreed. He always regretted that air mail pilots were
never issued flashy military-style uniforms. His feelings weren't
motivated by a sense of esprit de corps. He simply thought it would

significantly enhance his opportunity to meet women. He thought fancy garb and the "pilot" title was ideal, especially "with the girls."

Nearly 40 years after Eddie's death, Lipsner would write: "He was in his late twenties and did everything with a flourish and a style. Needless to say, the ladies of those days made quite a fuss over him — to which he didn't object." Indeed, Eddie enjoyed his "lover boy" image and he took care to dress the part.

Nearly all of the pilots saw themselves as great ladies' men, and it seemed like they would do anything for a date. In one instance, a young reserve pilot based in Bellefonte, Pennsylvania, had an engagement one evening with a young lady in New York. Despite his cautious plans he missed the eastbound train and began desperately searching for an alternative means of reaching New York. No other mail planes were available for such a lark. On the verge of despair, the flier's hopes were revived by the sounds of an incoming plane loaded with 35,000 letters mailed from west of the Mississippi River the day before. Although the assigned pilot would not turn over his flight to the rookie, he understood the young airman's plight and agreed to let him hitch a ride. This was a bit difficult, considering there wasn't a spare seat. Undaunted, the reserve pilot reportedly strapped his suitcase to one wing and lashed himself to the other and rode the wing for over 230 miles just to keep his appointment with his girl.

In 1918, dashing film star Douglas Fairbanks, Sr., made a unique proposition to the New York-based Harvey Fiske & Company brokerage firm. During the Fourth Liberty Loan drive, Fairbanks got the company to agree to purchase $1 million worth of Liberty Bonds if he could arrive at their New York office from Washington, D.C., in person, within five hours. Clad in Eddie Gardner's flight suit, commandeered for the occasion, Fairbanks was "mailed" to New York City. The "package" arrived in ample time.

Another romantically motivated incident initially baffled even Lipsner, who by late 1918 fully realized that his band would go to almost any extreme for a dalliance. "When one of his fliers began taking twice as long to cover the same distance as the reverse pilot, Dad got suspicious," recalled Lipsner's son Milton. "At first Dad chalked it up to wind currents, but that did not make sense, especially when he compared the gas consumption on the flights in both directions. They were about the same. Dad had the offending pilot tailed. Just as he suspected, the pilot was stopping en route to spend time with a girlfriend," Lipsner's son recounted.

Mrs. Lipsner hated that kind of alley cat conduct, fearing that it reflected poorly on her husband's management ability and jeopardized his efforts to improve the service. Captain Lipsner didn't much care for his pilots' antics either, but there wasn't much he could do if the fliers were on their own time.

Mrs. Lipsner wanted to distance her husband's personal life from

Wearing his trademark outfit, Eddie poses beside his plane with Frank Tower (on the right), a boyhood pal from Plainfield. The pilot's leather jacket and leggings included borrowings from the mounted soldiers of the day — at times even extending to a pair of spurs.

his professional work. She insisted that her husband not associate with his airmen after hours. They were a rougher and rowdier bunch, and he had a station in society to uphold. She made it her duty to maintain that separation. "As a rule, Dad never socialized with his pilots. Mom strictly enforced that edict," remembered son Jerry.

Although Lipsner would not associate with his subordinates after quitting time, he never stopped worrying about them. "He was overly concerned about their well being because they weren't altogether right, you know. They all had to be a bit crazy to do what they did and Dad knew it," said Milton.

Milton Lipsner also remembered how proud his father was of his pilots' safety record during his tenure. "He would rather reasonably delay a flight than risk a pilot's life." This wasn't an easy thing for a man like Lipsner. He was a fanatic when it came to punctuality. "If he said he would be somewhere at a specific time, he meant it … and if you were to meet him there, you had better be there at the exact time too," claimed his daughter-in-law. On this score, oddly enough Mrs. Lipsner was the exact opposite, which drove her husband crazy. "She was always late, if she arrived at all," remembered Milton Lipsner.

In many ways Lipsner was unlike his airmen. The dichotomy was so pronounced that it was amazing that there was any chemistry between them. They were usually coarse; he was refined. They were generally poorly educated; he excelled in college. They dressed casually; he was always impeccably attired — another point his wife insisted upon. She was like an obsessed stage mother, always looking out for her star performer, and sometimes imposing her own quirks. "She had a thing about ties," said son Jerry. "If it didn't have red in it, in her opinion, it wasn't a tie." And she didn't mind spending money. "If it was a question of necessities versus luxuries, the luxuries won every time," he recalled.

Eddie of course hated to dress up. He seldom wore a fashionable tie, and even when he did, it was usually badly rumpled. He preferred his airmen's attire, even when off duty.

The bond between Lipsner and Eddie nevertheless was especially strong, perhaps because each was somehow secretly what the other longed to become: Lipsner a bit more reckless; Eddie a bit more polished. But probably neither man would have been comfortable in a Prince-and-the-Pauper switch. Their psyches were not suited for anything but the roles they played in life. Lipsner could never have stopped planning for the future, and Eddie could never imagine living life other than one day at a time. For Lipsner, image was everything and ability was a close second. For Eddie, it was the other way around.

Their different outlooks on life were colored no doubt by their marital status. Lipsner was a contented husband while, at least to his friends, Eddie was a confirmed bachelor. He loved that image of himself, although in reality he had been married once. Few knew of his marriage to Edna Shafer in the early 1900s. It was something he kept well hidden, perhaps because the marriage only lasted a matter of months.

Ferne Spangler Bronk, now in her nineties, remembered how much her Aunt Edna loved her pilot boyfriend. But as she recalled, "Eddie didn't make much of a home for her, and the domineering personality of his mother made it an unsuccessful marriage." The wedding ceremony, which Mrs. Bronk described as "a very fashionable wedding for Plainfield," took place in the home of Eddie's sister on Center Street, the same place where his funeral service would be later years held.

By the time he reached 30, with one failed marriage behind him, Eddie began to doubt if he would ever find a suitable mate. Maybe he was getting too picky, or perhaps he wasn't meant for marriage. He confided in his sister: "I'm looking for hens now instead of chickens, but (the search) keeps me pretty busy with both. I make up my mind for a chicken and then I change my mind and think I can't be bothered."

Eddie found the women in Washington, D.C., especially possessive. "If you take one to a show or supper they start talking about furnishing a home or where we could live," he told his sister in 1919. "You would laugh if you were here," he told her. "Sometimes it's a joke. They think 'cause you're a flier you're a little time Jesus, or nutty I guess, and easy to grab. Not me, I'm gone then."

Whenever women got too close to Eddie, he would tell them he intended to live in the air and if they could stand that, then "I am for them." With a line like that, it's no wonder he never got any serious takers.

He did assure his sister that if one of her unmarried male in-laws would come to Washington and don a flight jacket and jodhpurs he'd be married in minutes. "I will loan him a flying suit and he can do the rest," Eddie wrote.

To say that Eddie had a roving eye — or hand, heart, or other body part for that matter — would be an understatement. Conquests counted more than closeness, and his transient lifestyle doomed him from establishing any strong, intimate bonds with anyone other than his immediate family. Eddie was like an Irish setter, always prone to roam at the first available moment. He figured he would settle down some day, but he didn't reckon on dying first.

His sister Nellie was his closest female confidant, but even his exchanges with her were sometimes guarded and often superficial, seldom soul searching or contemplative. In his letters, he would fill her in on the latest news or one of his recent aerial escapades. Only on few occasions did his letters hint at his own longings and personal trepidations.

He loved writing to his sister and often scribbled notes to her in the cockpit during his flight. He would drop some of these missives over the town of Plainfield with the certain knowledge that the hometown folk would make sure his notes were safely delivered. One of his airborne messages read: "Hello Sis and all. I am just out on a test flight and can't land. Everything is fine. Broke all records yesterday. Made it from Cleveland [to Chicago] in 2 hours 28 minutes, 335 miles. My motor went dead at 47th Street, but made my field o.k. Will be in Chicago Sun[day], leave Mon[day]. Regards to all."

Another of his cockpit letters to his sister simply read: "Just a line from the air. Out on a test flight or would land. Can't do much with this tub or would give you a thrill."

Not all of his letters were as lighthearted. "We lost one of our mechanics the other day," began one letter. "He was cranking one of the ships and slipped and fell into the propeller, but he didn't know what hit him. He died in about 15 minutes," Eddie wrote. The dead mechanic was Auguste Thiele, who sustained a fractured skull at 3:20 p.m., January 7, 1919. By 4:40 that afternoon he had been taken to a local hospital, where he died at 6:14 p.m.

CHAPTER TEN

PRONE TO TALES

Although Eddie set a remarkable record as an early aviator, his aerial accomplishments weren't always perfect. But like many pilots, he would compensate for any deficiencies with slight exaggerations. In 1919 he told his sister, "I still hold my 100 percent [record] in flying. I haven't missed or failed a trip. I am the only one that can say that." The following year he more accurately confessed, saying "I made my time schedule 97 percent of the time." But, as he said, he went through hell setting that level of performance. "I have hit everything from sunshine to tornadoes. Snow and rain is like a Sunday dinner now, only you don't enjoy it so much."

More than likely the tale about his run-in with a tornado was embellished a bit. The way Eddie told it, the incident occurred near Gage, Oklahoma, in 1918. He and his mechanic had just left Wichita, Kansas, when they encountered a violent rainstorm. Being short on fuel, Eddie thought it wise to gas up in the event things got worse further on. As they started down, they sighted a swirling conical-shaped cloud. In an instant the plane was sucked into the snaking storm. The powerful whirlwind thrashed the craft about, hurling it upward at tremendous speeds.

Finally the tornado broke up, but for more than a quarter of an hour the plane was at the mercy of the elements. The craft was buffeted in every direction, dipping so close to the ground that Eddie was certain his end had come. Only feet from the earth, his plane suddenly was jerked aloft like a glider caught in some titanic vacuum. When the plane plummeted to within 100 feet of the ground, the atmosphere abruptly grew calm. In an instant, Eddie seized control of his plane and guided it safely to earth. Eddie said he was never more thankful to get out of the plane with all his body parts still intact.

As the son of a flatland farmer, Eddie surely had seen his fair share of twisters while growing up. Plainfield was after all prime tornado territory. The flatness of Will County makes it especially vulnerable to the violent winds. Eddie was away in March 1920 when the last big tornado during his lifetime ripped through the area, destroying several farm buildings and orchards north of town. Fortunately, this one missed the Gardner farm, touching down instead on a tract a few farms away.

CHAPTER ELEVEN

FLY OR BE FIRED

L ipsner had been spoiled by the Army's fair-weather flying philosophy. "In the military service at that time, no pilot could be ordered to leave the ground. He flew only when he thought it was safe to fly," Lipsner wrote years later. But that attitude could not strictly apply to the Air Mail Service because some semblance of a schedule had to be maintained. Instead, Lipsner's belief was that if it was at all possible, the mail would go through, but he noted, "The actual decision as to whether a flight went up or not was open to debate between the pilot and the field superintendent." Lipsner insisted that such decisions be taken seriously. He told his pilots, "I don't expect you to do the impossible, but I do expect you to go up if there's the slightest chance that you can get through."

Praeger, however, had no such spirit of democracy. To him, the decision to fly was not open to debate; he insisted that his pilots fly no matter what! Like objects on a collision course, Praeger and Lipsner would eventually clash over who had the right to decide when to fly, and not surprisingly Eddie would be the at the center of the battle. The incident would foreshadow Lipsner's resignation one month later.

Although Lipsner thought Eddie was his finest pilot, Praeger soon would have a different opinion. Crazy though he appeared at times, Eddie did have some limits. His willingness to try almost anything was reached on November 18, 1918.

If an airman wished to survive, he practiced all the time and quickly learned his limits. In an interview with Robert S. Gallagher, published in *American Heritage* in 1974, air ace Jimmy Doolittle discussed this crucial self-enlightenment. According to Doolittle:

> You see, everything I ever did in aviation I practiced and practiced and practiced. As a result I was able to do things that appeared rather hazardous to someone who hadn't

done them. Let me give you a better example of this. When I was the Army's chief test pilot at old McCook Field [at Dayton, Ohio] in 1927, I practiced flying the route from Dayton to Moundsville, time after time, until I had memorized every windmill, every telephone pole, every silo, and every farmhouse, so that I could fly under weather conditions where other pilots, much better pilots than I, could not fly. Yet when my commanding officer heard about it, he grounded me for being in his opinion too irresponsible, and I lost the job I enjoyed more than any job I ever had. A few years later I was flying from Cleveland to New York in bad weather. In those days they had revolving beacons every ten miles. Well, I missed a beacon and made an emergency landing. Soon a farmer came along and informed me that the next beacon was out of order, which explained why I had missed it. Then the farmer said, by the way, the mail just went over. It was a matter of pride to me then not to let anyone fly when I couldn't, but I realized that the reason the mail had gone through was that the pilot knew that terrain so well, just as I had known the area around McCook Field. So I stayed on the ground, and I have always thought that perhaps that was the day I became a good flier, because that day I learned my limitations.

Among the flying fraternity that simple rule to survival — know your limits — was essential. You knew your limits and lived, or you exceeded your limits and sometimes died.

But following the rule often amounted to a case of "do as I say, not as I do." Pilots were by nature inclined to take risks or show off. And even those who knew their limits and were content to fly within them died anyway, but perhaps not in as great a number as those who constantly stretched themselves.

Had Eddie chosen to fly always within his limits, perhaps he would have lived to write his autobiography after a long, successful career. Instead, he consistently chose to push himself well beyond the limits of his proficiency. This was another of his flaws … ultimately a mortal one.

On the morning of November 18, 1918, Eddie learned something about his limits, although the full impact of that lesson somehow failed to sink in. He awoke at Belmont Park to find conditions impossible for flying. Yet, at the urging of the station manager, he nervously toyed with the idea of going aloft, after all he had flown in soupy fog before; perhaps he could fly above it. After a bit more coaxing, he gave in. But once airborne, he realized that he had made a potentially deadly mistake. This time the fog was blinding at every altitude he tried, so bad that he was forced to grope his way to safety as best he could. As it was, he landed a good distance from his starting point, but at least he was down safely.

The engine had barely cooled down when he was ordered by the air station's manager to get back into the cockpit and try again. After what he had just been through, Eddie chose to ignore such idiotic demands. While his refusal might have been acceptable to Lipsner, it wasn't okay with Second Assistant Postmaster General Praeger. He was livid at Eddie's insubordination. He cabled New York demanding that he or any other available pilot "start the mail without a minute's delay."

Sheepishly, the operations chief at Belmont Park wired Praeger: "Replying to your telegram to start the mail without a minute's delay, have consulted Gardner and [Robert] Shank and both refuse to fly on account of weather conditions here." A few minutes later the station manager also telegraphed Lipsner with the same bad news, adding "Both [Gardner and Shank] feel it would be suicide to attempt flight." Lipsner agreed that as soon as there was a break in the weather, either Eddie or Shank would fly. At the same time, Lipsner also gave orders to halt the northbound progress of pilot Dana C. "Daddy" DeHart, flying inbound toward Belmont Park. According to the New York field superintendent, "If (the) fog remains as it is DeHart will never land here." Lipsner had to hastily check DeHart, halting him like a runner about to steal a base, holding him up at Bustleton, Pennsylvania, until the fog cleared.

Within a few anxious minutes everything was settled, with no real damage done. Eddie and Shank were about to fly, and DeHart was safely holed up in Pennsylvania.

Unfortunately however, Praeger, an autocratic, cigar-smoking former newspaperman, was out for blood. To his way of thinking, no one had the right to refuse to carry out one of his orders and keep their job. Without consulting Lipsner, he fired Eddie and Shanks on the spot.

When word of the firings reached Lipsner — who had been absent from his Washington office for several weeks while scouting out the possibility of creating an air mail route in Minnesota — he was livid. Praeger had given the boot to the airmen Lipsner called "my top pilots."

In a letter to a friend, Eddie recorded the events that led to his discharge: "I attempted a flight and lost sight of [the] ground at 25 feet. I was lost for 35 minutes, but by careful flying and good luck, landed safely 5 miles from Belmont aerial station."

Lipsner protested the sackings, but once again Praeger stuck to his guns. As far as he was concerned, his action was a prerogative of rank. Under much of the Praeger regime, the Post Office Department would have a "fly or be fired" philosophy. The tough-minded Praeger firmly believed that visibility wasn't essential. He thought that any pilot worth his salt should be able to fly by a compass.

Praeger's position was totally unrealistic for the times. Most of his pilots simply didn't have much faith in instrument flying. They considered it less risky to rely on their skills and instincts. Charles Lindbergh once described instrument flying as putting one's faith in "untrusted needles, falling, leaning right and left."

Years later, James Doolittle's opinion was that most early pilots either "couldn't fly by instruments or didn't believe in them." Doolittle believed that the problem was compounded by the attitude of the airmen. "Too many pilots had contempt for the weather and thought it was a blight on their reputations if they refused to make an attempt to reach their destination," he observed in his 1991 autobiography. As an aviation pioneer himself, Doolittle thought that "too often, pilots would fly into steadily worsening conditions and encounter situations where they couldn't turn back and had only two choices left: bail out (if they wore a parachute) or try to luck it through."

Later airmen learned from Eddie's mistake. They knew that although they'd be fired like he had been for refusing to fly in foul weather, nothing would be done to them if they reported "engine trouble." Praeger was soon amazed at the high correlation between "engine trouble" and severe weather conditions. On extremely inclement days, most if not all the planes at certain fields miraculously seemed to suffer mechanical problems.

Thanks to Praeger's rigid insistence that pilots fly under any weather conditions, a number of good pilots either lost their jobs or

DH-4s, like the one shown here, were modified so that air mail pilots flew from the rear cockpit, as far as possible from the fuel tanks. World War I pilots labeled the DH-4s "flaming coffins" because they caught fire so easily.

their lives.

Although in 1918 the service's few pilots were unprepared to face Praeger in a full-blown confrontation, within a year their growing numbers made them more confident. By the summer of 1919 they began to flex their collective muscle. Initially, at Praeger's insistence, flights were attempted with less than a 50-foot visibility, which didn't allow much maneuvering room to find a safe landing place if something went wrong, especially if the aircraft was over an urban area. The pilots hammered away at this issue and eventually won some concessions, revealing the first real chink in Praeger's armor, which they were quick to exploit.

Praeger gave in a bit by accepting, at least in principle, that there was a ceiling under which pilots would not be expected to fly. If visibility were below 200 feet, the pilots did not have to fly. In time, conditions improved even more. By the early 1920s, a "Safety First" philosophy had replaced the "fly under any circumstances" mentality. The safe flying program did much to reduce the death toll, as did technical innovations.

Although Praeger had fired Eddie, Lipsner still harbored notions of somehow rehiring his ace pilot. He especially wanted Eddie to fly a Handley-Paige. When Lipsner visited Eddie, who was heartbroken over his dismissal, the pilot begged him to use his pull to get his job back. But by then Lipsner himself was beginning to doubt how long he'd be superintendent of the Air Mail Service. Praeger was appointing people to air mail positions without even consulting with Lipsner.

Several years later, Lipsner wrote: "I was furious at the whole thing, and thoroughly disgusted at this interference. I saw clearly that if political influence was going to run this service, then it wasn't for me any more." Lipsner told Eddie to simply go home and forget the whole thing for awhile. He told him he was working on some other ventures and would make sure that his buddy was a part of his plans.

Lipsner ultimately resigned in December 1918. Expressing his solidarity with Lipsner, Miller resigned as well. His resignation letter was a vote of no confidence in Praeger. Miller wrote:

> Being in full sympathy with Captain B.B. Lipsner, superintendent of the Air Mail Service, in his opinion as to the contemplated reorganization plans for the Air Mail Service, I am frank to state that I do not feel confident in the outcome of a plan different from the one which is now being successfully operated and knowing full well Captain Lipsner's capabilities of directing the Air Mail Service to a successful conclusion to date. Therefore, it is obvious that I use my best judgment and take the stand of handing herewith my resignation.

The loss of Miller was a real blow to Praeger, who needed experi-

Night flying was essential to realize the full potential of air mail. Landing lights developed in the 1920s offset some of the hazards associated with night flying with primitive navigational aids.

enced pilots. He wasn't prepared for such wholesale defection. He immediately began working on Miller to change his mind, offering vague promises that he would bring Shanks and Eddie back as well.

Again Lipsner turned to the media to tell his side of the story. He told the press how during his 111-day tenure as the head of the Air Mail Service the system was getting better and better. During that period he said that it had suffered only two failed trips on account of bad weather and three on account of accidents. There additionally were seven forced landings, but all that was before November, which, according to Lipsner was the service's best month to date. "In November we operated a perfect month without any failures, showing conclusively that the service under my supervision had reached and was maintaining a record of 100-percent efficiency."

Lipsner of course didn't include in his calculations the aborted flight that had resulted in Eddie's sacking, reasoning that it would have gone off the minute the conditions cleared, if only Praeger left well enough alone. But if November marked the beginning of the Air Mail Service's perfect flying record, it also marked the beginning of the end for Lipsner's position with the service.

Eventually, Praeger succeeded in enticing Miller back in to the fold, and soon others followed his lead. On December 27, 1918, Miller broke the news to Lipsner, who by then was no longer on the postal service payroll. "[Gardner] flew to New York yesterday and I think he is coming back again. Today, they also sent for Bob (Shank). He is in North Carolina. I have not seen Ed yet so I don't know whether he is going to stay or not." As it turned out, Eddie would return to the Air Mail Service, but not for very long!

In hindsight, there was no way Eddie could have stayed with the new organization under Praeger. He had at least three things going against him: he was too closely associated with Lipsner for Praeger to ever trust him fully; he had been insubordinate to Praeger; and soon his skills would no longer be in short supply.

By Christmas of 1920, 5,000 applications for air mail pilot positions were on file, from which 2,500 were tested. Of those given examinations, only 225 were appointed, and 50 of them were summarily discharged for insubordination.

The biggest cause for the firings was the constant temptation to show off, just like Eddie. New pilots were especially likely to perform stunts in front of their colleagues, thrilling residents near the landing fields. But their foolishness failed to impress their superiors. As the *New York Times* observed, "They had failed to consider themselves as racing car drivers transferred to trucks, none the less important and involving just as much skill, but not so frisky."

In addition to his connections to Lipsner, his insubordination, and the flood of new pilots, there was another, more fundamental reason why Eddie would have to move on. Once a pilot attained the maximum flying time to qualify for the highest level of pay, which Eddie had by 1919, he could no longer expect additional raises. At that point the older pilots were expected to step back or disappear, permitting the younger fliers to be promoted. Although this was a noble practice, it had a detrimental impact upon service. Schedules were often interrupted because the younger pilots lacked the essential skills needed to fly under all sorts of conditions. To overcome this problem, the pay scheme was ultimately changed so that salaries ranged from $5,000 to $7,500 a year.

If the seemingly endless supply of potential pilots was good news for Praeger, any elation he felt should have been tempered by the fact that the strong-willed Texan was actually strangling the service in his attempt to squeeze greater efficiency out of it. Morale meant nothing to Praeger and neither did tenure. In his view the system was grossly inefficient. He wanted to force postal employees to work longer and harder — at no additional cost — and he particularly wanted its older workers to resign. It was charged that Praeger especially wanted to get rid of all old-time Republicans, which was somewhat true, as well as all Union Army veterans, which was never really proven, although the unsympathetic press had a field day with that assertion. The outrage was captured by the *Baldwin City* (Kansas) *Ledger,* which observed that Praeger "recently attracted nationwide attention by the wholesale manner in which he decapitated clerks and carriers in the Washington (D.C.) post office [where he had served as postmaster before being asked to serve as second assistant postmaster general] who were found guilty of wearing the old bronze button and in connection therewith having given too many years of faithful service to Uncle Sam." According to the paper, "Protests from Grand Army of the Republic posts were of no avail, for their voting strength is not as great as it used to be and the South is strictly in the saddle."

Cynically, the media noted that Praeger's actions made good financial sense and, in a cold way, they did. Replacing older, $1,200 Republicans with good $800 Democrats was quite a savings. Reportedly Praeger saved as much as $90,000 in the cost of running the

Mail is being loaded into the forward compartment of a DeHavilland at Hadley Air Field, New Jersey, in 1925.

Washington post office. But he and Burleson were earning enemies. As soon as Praeger was appointed to the second assistant postmaster general's post, the press began to scream. Noted in newspapers in 1916, "the wily Burleson has finally found a man who can do great things in the postal service and the head of [Joseph] Stewart [who with 24 years of service with the Post Office Department was forced to resign] now falls into the basket to make way for Praeger."

None of the fliers was prepared to stand up to Praeger in 1918, especially Eddie. When it came to bureaucratic hardball, Eddie was out of Praeger's league. He finally left the Air Mail Service in 1919.

Eddie left at a time when conditions were improving. In 1918, during the Air Mail Service's first year of operation, engine failures were a constant problem. Lipsner calculated that the service had 37 engine-related forced landings — one for every 3,460 miles flown. The causes varied. Radiator problems and fouled spark plugs accounted for the greatest number of failures, with eight each. Oil leaks contributed to seven failures, while magneto troubles caused five. Leaking fuel lines, bad valves, and faulty carburetors each caused two in-flight failures. Exhaust valves also were a problem once the planes landed. They tended to warp if the engine wasn't properly allowed to cool down.

Rain, snow, and electrical storms also took their toll. During 1918, 51 pilots were brought down by weather. High winds were a large part of the problem, and in a few instances head winds were so fierce that, at the height of the gusts, planes were said to have literally been blown backwards.

Between 1918 and 1920 numerous innovations were introduced. To overcome the problems associated with vibrations affecting the spinning of directional compasses — the flaw which was blamed for George Boyle's poor performance in 1918 — the postal service developed a new ball-style compass. The Post Office Department also resolved the problem of fouling of spark plugs, which was especially problematic with the Liberty engines. The department hired an

The gradual establishment of emergency landing fields and lighted flyways and fields saved many an air mail flier whose fuel had run low.

inventor and gave him an engine as well as access to a flying field where he could conduct his experiments. By 1920, this problem had been resolved and self-cleaning spark plugs had become standard.

To make it easier for aviators to find landing sites in foggy weather, the postal service turned to the Bureau of Standards for help in creating a set of sirens and microphones that would allow the pilots to detect the amplified siren sounds above the roar of the engine. Much to the regret of local residents living within ear shot of the Air Mail Service's airfield at College Park, Maryland, the "seven step amplifier" made the siren sounds carry for miles. Unfortunately, the system did not work as well as expected. Pilots were not able to locate the airfield by this type of sound alone. According to an article in the April 3, 1920, issue of *The Independent,* this was overcome by the development of a device that alerted pilots "through a barrage of radio waves surrounding the field, just when he was above the center of the field." Upon arriving at this central point, the pilot could commence to spiral to the ground through the fog until he was in sight of land. This system wasn't totally flawless. For one thing, the initial wireless tower was 200 feet tall, a fatal obstacle when foggy weather limited a pilot's visual range. The tower height was reduced to 57 feet by 1920. In addition, a 20-foot-tall radio antennae at College Park gave off a signal that could be picked up 200 miles away.

Another important advancement was the Army's development of the reversible propeller. This enabled aircraft to stop within 200 feet of touching down, rather than the previous 800-foot roll out.

Despite numerous technological improvements and greater safety precautions, the pilots were limited to an air speed of 80 miles per hour. The mail planes could typically fly much faster than that, but postal officials believed aircraft engines lasted longer and operating costs were lower at the reduced speed.

CHAPTER TWELVE
BARNSTORMER'S MENTALITY

The routine flights between New York and Chicago included a brief stopover in Cleveland. In Cleveland, Eddie had another narrow escape while taking off on the morning of September 15, 1919, bound for Chicago. Unable to gain altitude, he tried to make an emergency landing in a vacant field adjacent to a cluster of homes. The helpless plane inched lower and lower, on a deadly course headed straight for a crowded street. Just then Eddie's craft swerved slightly away from the panic-stricken onlookers and took aim at two nearby homes. Sensing impending disaster, the pedestrians scattered. Like Chicken Littles, most average citizens tended to fear being squashed by falling airplanes. They envisioned being crushed, much like the Wicked Witch of the East was flattened by Dorothy's house in "The Wizard of Oz." To calm such fears, one brilliant mail service spokesman gave this advice: "Don't Run. You might as well try to run away from a bullet as an airplane. If the machine is swooping down, take a dive for the earth and snuggle up close. Then you're all right for the thing runs along the ground upon alighting, and even should the wheels crease your back, they wouldn't hurt." Not likely! The empty weight of a DeHavilland DH-4 or a Curtiss Jenny was approximately 1,800 pounds, the equivalent of being run over by a compact car.

In his own account, for the record, Eddie said: "I saw that I would have to land at once. I sighted a small open field beyond Parkhill Avenue and tried to bring my plane down there. This was only a few blocks from where I took [to] the air at Woodland Hills Park. I was only about a hundred feet in the air at the time, but I thought I might make the open lot. I was directly above the avenue when the engine suddenly stopped. I was then so near the ground, and my speed was so slight, that there was no chance to maneuver for a landing." The houses were just too close together.

The Flagg and Lotz houses following Eddie's crash in Cleveland, Ohio, in 1919.

Determining that his plane could not clear the tops of the houses, and knowing that his gas tank would almost certainly explode upon impact, Eddie decided to bail out, according to a local newspaper report. He wasn't wearing a parachute, but that wouldn't have mattered much since he did not have sufficient altitude to successfully deploy one anyway. Instead, the newspaper recounted how, as his plane skimmed the roof on one building, he jumped. A split-second later his plane reportedly ricocheted into the roof of the house next door. Eddie was said to have landed between the two buildings just as the gasoline tank blew up, sending flames and splintering wreckage everywhere.

But when the event was reported, accurately as it turned out, in another Cleveland newspaper, readers might have thought the papers were describing two totally separate accidents. Eddie didn't bail out. He stayed with his plane, even when it nosed into one of two houses. The homes were owned by Mrs. William Flagg and Mrs. Perry J. Lotz. Both women were alone in their homes at the time.

Eddie's plane grazed the Flagg house and struck the other full-force, impaling itself briefly. The weight of the tail-end section apparently broke the plane in two, just as the aircraft engine exploded. The force of the explosion blew the severed plane backwards. The wreckage dropped into the narrow yard between the two dwellings, with Eddie still strapped in his seat.

According to Eddie, as soon as the plane hit the ground, "I unstrapped myself from my belt. I did this as rapidly as I could and stepped clear of the wreck. A moment later there was a second explosion, worse than the first. The force of it blew me back, but again I escaped unhurt."

Witnesses said the second explosion blew the gasoline tank straight up into the air, hurling it well above the roof lines of the two damaged houses. Both women were working in their kitchens at the time of the accident. Neither was injured, nor were they mad as hornets, which was amazing, especially for Mrs. Lotz because the upper floor of her house was by then well toasted and about one-third of her roof was missing.

Mrs. Flagg was startled by the sound of the initial impact. "I could not guess what had happened," she told a newspaper reporter. "Then I smelled smoke. As soon as I realized something was afire I ran out [of the house]. There was the plane, or what was left of it, lying between the two houses." At that point the second explosion occurred. Mrs. Flagg dashed into the backyard to seize the garden hose in case there was a fire. She was still pouring a meager stream of water on both her house and the burning airplane when the fire department arrived.

Luckily, the two Lotz children, ages 7 and 11, were in school at the time. Had they been at home in their rooms upstairs when Eddie's surprise landing occurred, more than likely they would have lost their lives. Mrs. Lotz was cleaning the breakfast dishes at the time. "I was washing out a jar," she said, "[when] I heard the whirring of the airplane propeller. But that was nothing to attract my attention. We live so near the place where the mail planes land and start we hear them often. But this time the whirring sounded much louder than usual, and I knew the plane must be flying low. Then suddenly, the whirring stopped. I knew something was going to happen and I held my breath."

Mrs. Lotz ran to the back door to look out. As she did, the plane struck. She couldn't see the plane from her vantage point, which hit towards the front of her house, but she instinctively knew what had happened. Seconds later the first explosion shook the building. From where she was standing she could see bits of roofing shingles and wood showering down from the sky. She ran into her yard and saw Eddie climbing out of what was left of his plane.

Accounts differ about what happened after the crash. One version was that Eddie, only slightly bruised, gathered up what little bits of mail he could find from his 350-pound load and slowly made his way back to the airfield for another plane. Within a short time of narrowly escaping death, he reportedly was again winging his way towards Chicago.

Writing in 1961, Lester Bishop gave a different account of the incident. Bishop was an air mail pilot who served from December 27, 1918, to November 30, 1919. He returned to the mail service on

September 16, 1920, and continued until June 20, 1927. He first met Eddie in 1917 at Chanute Field, where Eddie was a flight instructor. Bishop said the two became fairly good friends. About the Cleveland crash, Bishop wrote: "As I was just across the street from where this happened and seen the whole affair, seen Turk jump out [of the plane following the crash] and run hell bent. He did not stop to [gather up] anything."

Even though he was nowhere near Cleveland at the time, Lipsner discounted Bishop's story. Still defending his by then long-dead ace airman, Lipsner dismissed Bishop's account, labeling it "Sour Grapes — [Bishop] hoped he could have been one of the original four [air mail pilots, but] Gardner was a better pilot than he was." Bishop's remarks don't hold up for another reason as well. Photographs exist of Eddie standing beside his wrecked plane. Had he run off moments after the crash, he wouldn't have been around for the photo opportunity.

While in hindsight the wreck was somewhat comical, the local politicians weren't laughing. There was nothing funny about their constituents' houses going up in flames. Voters don't care much for that sort of thing. Immediately the town council made a showing of concern. They swiftly created a special three-man committee to study what other communities were doing to protect themselves from falling air mail planes. Another resolution, proposed by Councilman Frank Soika, called for the closing of the air station altogether if the town was not satisfied with future safeguards. In support of his motion, Soika said, "Numerous accidents have resulted and there is much poison from the testing of [engines]." Soika also felt a bit betrayed over what had become of the airfield. "The field was given to the government as a place for landing mail planes, but recently others have taken advantage of the field and have charged to take passengers up," he complained. The council's actions produced no significant results.

Little also came of a proposal advanced by the Cleveland Aviation Club to line all air mail sacks with asbestos to prevent the contents from burning.

The mail Eddie was carrying on that ill-fated Cleveland takeoff bore the signs of his crash. Most of the letters were toasted around the edges and water damaged. To explain the damage, Cleveland's postmaster had little notes hastily printed. "Accompanying mail was unavoidably damaged by fire on areoplane [sic] due to leave Cleveland, Ohio, at 9:30 a.m., Sept. 15, 1919," was all the notes said. An apology apparently was not deemed necessary.

Amazed that he hadn't been hurt, Eddie felt himself all over to make sure he wasn't missing anything. Outwardly, there wasn't as much as a scratch on him as far as he could tell. His clothes weren't even too badly soiled. But what about his nerves? According to his friend Lipsner, "This experience would have been enough to stop most pilots, but such trifles hardly touched the surface of Gardner's nerves."

His plane however — a DeHavilland DH-4 — was totally demolished.

Jack Knight flew a DeHavilland, and his story is one of the most dramatic in the annals of those early aviators. Knight's odyssey began on a February evening in 1921. He was scheduled to fly the North Platte-to-Omaha leg of a special, 2,629-mile transcontinental flight, intended to demonstrate the value of round-the-clock relays. Darkness fell during the Cheyenne-North Platte leg of the eastbound flight, and the plane landed by the light of bonfires. Knight took over the mail and headed for Omaha. Around midnight, near Kearney, Nebraska, he encountered snow. Landing at Omaha by the light of burning gasoline drums placed along the runway, Knight found that his relief pilot had not arrived. By this time the snowfall had become a blizzard.

After refueling his plane, Knight took off for Chicago at 2:00 a.m. with only a highway map to guide him over terrain he had never flown before. Deep snow covered the airfield at Des Moines, preventing his landing, so Knight put down at an emergency landing site at Iowa City, Iowa. He was forced to make the landing by the light of railroad flares that had been set out by the night watchman, the field's lone attendant.

Knight laboriously refueled his plane himself and then took off again, heading toward Lake Michigan, which he was sure would enable him to locate Chicago. Along the way the snow stopped, only to be replaced by fog. Finally, with daybreak, the fog lifted and Lake Michigan came into view. When Knight landed at Chicago's "Checkerboard Field" he was greeted by a throng of people who had gathered to see if the daring young pilot would finish his remarkable flight. His mail was relayed on to Cleveland and then New York,

Eddie's flight helmet. On one side he penned his initials, on the other he wrote "Turk." Although "Turk" and "Turk Bird" were acceptable nicknames, to his mother and sister he was always "Ed."

finally arriving 33 hours and 20 minutes after leaving San Francisco. This feat helped ensure the continuation of Air Mail Service and made Knight a national hero. He saved the first continuous coast-to-coast air mail flight from certain failure, despite the fact that he had broken his nose a few days earlier in a plane crash.

By November 1921, ten radio stations were installed at principal airfields along the New York-to-San Francisco flyway so that accurate weather forecasts could be transmitted to the airfields. In addition, within a few years other innovations appeared, including radio phones, which were installed aboard mail planes, and parachute flares, which were placed in the underbellies of many mail planes, allowing pilots to illuminate a landing site when forced to make an emergency landing. Giant beacon lamps, mounted atop tall towers, were erected along the principal east-west flyway at 25- and 30-mile intervals to mark emergency landing fields in case pilots got into trouble. Powerful searchlights were also installed at all regular runways to facilitate night flying, and airfield boundary lights were set out. By 1925, 61 of the Post Office Department's 96 mail planes were equipped with landing lights for night flying.

By 1924 scheduled air mail service between New York and San Francisco routinely required only 34 hours. The Post Office Department got out of the business of flying the mail in the 1920s, turning that responsibility over to commercial air carriers. Postal officials had long realized that there would come a time when private interests would take over mail flights. Commercial carriers were developing feasible routes or covering the same flyways as air mail planes. For the burgeoning airlines, contracts for hauling mail helped to offset meager or nonexistent passenger revenues.

CHAPTER THIRTEEN

"I AM STILL GOING HIGHER"

I Am Still Going Higher" comprised Eddie's simple Christmas message to his friends in 1919. He had recently changed jobs and was now working for a Lincoln, Nebraska, company — the Nebraska Aircraft Corporation — demonstrating planes, promoting sales, conducting aerial tests, and ferrying planes to buyers. Eddie capitalized on his connections with the executives at the Standard Aircraft Corporation to land the Midwest-based job.

Nebraska Aircraft bought up the Army's stockpile of Standard J-I aircraft after the war and gave them a make-over, transforming them into pleasure and commercial craft. The company also cornered much of the market of surplus Standard aircraft parts, buying up large quantities housed at Ellington Field and other government warehouses. Purchases also included 166 Hispano-Suiza engines.

In addition to the Army aircraft, Nebraska Aircraft also acquired the factory and inventory of the Standard Aircraft Corporation in Elizabeth, New Jersey.

To help expand Nebraska Aircraft's sales, Eddie was dispatched to Texas to demonstrate the company's planes and entice someone into becoming the firm's Texas distributor.

While in the Lone Star State, Eddie did some "good deed" flying over the flood-ridden Trinity River. "E.V. Gardinier [sic] piloted the ship over the flooded bottoms Wednesday almost all day observing the flood waters and hunting for any person who might be marooned or in danger," observed the *Dallas Times.* The mercy flights were arranged by Lewis Robinson, the vice president of the newly organized Texas branch of the Nebraska Aircraft Corporation. Robinson's company used Standard planes as part of its aerial taxi service, carrying passengers for short flights to any part of the huge state.

During most such trips Ira Biffle accompanied Eddie. Like Eddie, Biffle was a former air mail pilot. Lipsner had hired Biffle shortly after the Chicago-to-New York Pathfinding Flights, along with nine others. Lipsner was always proud of the fact that he had convinced Biffle to come aboard since, as Lipsner said, "Biffle was the man who taught Lindbergh to fly. And Lindbergh, who later became an air mail pilot himself, flying between St. Louis and Chicago, called him a very tough instructor."

Of the duo, Eddie typically piloted a Standard Tourabout, while Biffle commanded a Standard Speedster during their exhibition flights.

For someone with Eddie's degree of flash and wanderlust, the job with Nebraska Aircraft was ideal. Now he could travel to air shows around the country, living the romantic life of an aerial charioteer, all at the company's expense. Indeed, many other pilots of his generation were barnstorming around the country, having a grand time demonstrating the latest flying machines. But Eddie's position wasn't entirely a boondoggle. Few of his contemporaries knew the Standard as well as he did; he was the plane's best spokesperson.

As part of his new job, he completed a long-distance flight from Lincoln to Mexico City, with stops at Junction City, Kansas; Liberal, Kansas; Tucumcari, New Mexico; El Paso, Texas; and Chihuahua, Jimenez, Toucon, Saltillo, and San Louis Potosi, Mexico. Part of that record-setting flight required him to fly above snow-covered mountain peaks, soaring at an altitude of 16,000 feet. This is what Eddie meant when he wrote, "I am still going higher."

Posing here in Saltillo, Mexico, Eddie loved to show off his Nebraska Aircraft Corporation Standard Tourabout to potential buyers.

On the ground, the weather in January 1919 was quite mild, with very little snow and only a few exceptionally bone-chilling days. But aloft, it was a different story. On one trip to New York, Eddie recorded temperatures of 24°F. In a letter to his sister, he described his

flights as "fine sleigh riding around on these clouds, but I didn't feel the cold." It's no wonder! He was wearing his usual flying gear, and an additional heavy leather vest and coat. On top of this he was wrapped in a one-piece leather flying suit. And, for added protection, an outer layer consisted of a one-piece fur-lined electric-heated suit, with sheepskin boots and electrically heated socks. He also wore a pair of high overshoes and heated mittens. His head was capped with a fur helmet and his face was covered with a leather mask, with beady slits for eyes. With all that on it's a wonder he was even able to squeeze into the cramped little cockpit. He certainly must have looked for all the world like an overstuffed walrus.

To protect his face from the effects of flying in an open cockpit, Eddie used this leather face mask.

Eddie enjoyed the part of his job with the Nebraska Aircraft Corporation that required him to wow the crowds at air shows. It was risky business, but he loved stunt flying and he especially relished every chance he got to astonish the crowds of onlookers in his gleaming white Standard Tourabout airplane. He thrived on the transient adulation.

But not everyone appreciated his aerial antics. When it was announced that Eddie would conduct stunts over one Nebraska town, city officials went into a tizzy. One local commissioner assured anxious town folk that trick flying above the city would result in swift legislation against the operation of airplanes within city limits. The mayor held a similar view and said that even if the organizers of the flights backed down, it was only a matter of time before some such ordinance was passed.

Eddie didn't help matters much when he announced plans to land right in the middle of town. This infuriated the chief of police, who angrily announced plans to arrest the mischievous pilot the minute he touched down. A far as the chief was concerned, passing an airplane ordinance after the fact was useless. All he wanted to know was how far up in the air his police powers extended; and, if he had aerial jurisdiction, how was he going to catch the pilot.

Even with all the "official" furor, the sponsors of the air show, the Colonial Orchestra, upped the ante with a small-town media blitz. Ads in the local newspaper announced the three-day air show and promised spectators more than just aerial entertainment: "E.V. Gardner of the Nebraska Aircraft Corporation will thrill you with his stunts in a Lincoln made plane over 15th and O [Streets], after which he will make a landing on 15th Street, Thursday at Noon." As an incentive to be on hand to witness the landing, readers were advised that "Daredevil Gardner will throw our cards from his plane Thursday Noon and the first fifty to be taken to the office of *The Daily Star* will be given free tickets to see ['The Great Air Robbery']."

True to his promise, Eddie startled the towns folks and officials alike by landing in front of the Colonial Theater in the heart of the city. He then got out of town fast.

In August 1920, Eddie put his Standard Tourabout through its paces at the premier Wisconsin air derby. Eddie's plane was entered by Thomas Hamilton of the Hamilton Aero Manufacturing Company on behalf of the *Milwaukee Journal.*

The course covered 264 miles running from Milwaukee via an inland route near Fond du Lac. Entrants in the derby were handicapped because of the different factory speeds of the various planes.

The winning time was two hours and 25 minutes. The winning pilot was Eddie Gardner, taking a purse of $700 and the Wisconsin State Pilots Championship Cup. The *Journal* presented a trophy to the Aero Club of Wisconsin in honor of Eddie's feat and in recognition of the fact that Eddie was one of the club's members.

Unlike the other contestants, Eddie was at a slight disadvantage. He had a passenger on board during the race, Muriel Kelly. She was a *Journal* reporter assigned to cover the race firsthand. Her employer credited her as "the first woman to participate as a passenger in an air derby in America."

Miss Kelly got airsick almost as soon as the race began. She almost gave up after Eddie completed the first leg of the race to Kenosha. Her discomfort must have showed because one of the officials asked her if she wanted to go on when the plane got back to Milwaukee. "Right then I determined that the first woman to fly in an air derby wasn't going to let seasickness stop her," she reported to her readers. Other than that, her only real problem was the engine noise. "The first sensation I had, besides that of going up in the air, was that someone had mistaken my head for a drum. The noise was terrific, but in spite of everything I was not afraid."

The *Journal* attributed Eddie's success to "expert manipulation of the machine and an intimate knowledge of air currents."

It was somewhat surprising that Eddie did as well as he did, given that he had arrived at the derby at the very last minute after having flown about 600 miles from Nebraska with the worst passenger he'd ever had — a pig.

Eddie had given a free lift to a plump porker named "Cornhusker." The pig was a gift from

Always willing to take a lady for a ride, Eddie took Muriel Kelly aloft for 264-mile race from Milwaukee in 1920. Unaccustomed to flying, Miss Kelly got airsick almost immediately.

the University of Nebraska's agricultural college and Nebraska's Governor, S.R. McKelvie, to the Governor of Wisconsin. In turning over the terrified swine at the conclusion of the long flight, Eddie's only comment was, "Ol' Cornhusker sure enjoyed the scenery coming in from the west." But Eddie hated the flight. Apparently Cornhusker struggled all the way, snorting and squealing incessantly and making it impossible for the pilot to hear the intricate sounds of the engine.

After his triumphant finish at the race that day, Eddie flew demonstration hourly flights over the fairgrounds.

CHAPTER FOURTEEN

THE NINTH LIFE

Eddie was always welcomed as his sister's home. He would visit her two-story farmhouse, which was shaped like a reclining "T," as often as possible. After Martin Gardner's death in 1915, the tidy Spangler household, with its two fenced side yards, had become more than just a convenient spot for the air ace to stay. It was his emotional anchor, especially after his mother remarried and moved to Joliet.

But the Spangler farm — with its large out buildings located across Taylor Road from the main house where the farm pigs, cows and horses were stabled — also served as a vivid reminder of what Eddie had worked so hard to escape. From an early age he had wanted nothing to do with farm work, and his sister's farm only served to reinforce that conviction.

While Eddie was always welcomed, his comings and goings were not always appreciated. Clayton Eaton, who had married Eddie's niece Evelyn, recalled how the "great man" would drop into and out of his future wife's family's life, stopping in for occasional visits on holidays and birthdays. His visits were sporadic and brief. More often as not he stayed only an hour or two before disappearing again. This transience didn't always sit well with his sister, who began to look upon him as something of a highly paid aerial hobo.

On Sunday, August 22, 1920, Eddie and an old air mail buddy, Frank Tower, flew into Plainfield at 4 p.m. Tower, who was also raised around Plainfield, had served as chief mechanic in charge of the College Park, Maryland, airfield. He had been one of Eddie's boyhood pals, and they were especially close. Tower was a toe taller than Eddie and somewhat better looking; but with respect to their attire, both were nearly identical in their riding pants, leggings, and leather flying jackets. Both had taken up flying at about the same time; but, unlike Eddie, Tower would ultimately settle down with a wife.

For Eddie, this visit home was like many previous trips. The flight

93

down from Chicago took only about 20 minutes, but more and more each trip was like a voyage back in time. In Eddie's mind, the minutes in the air probably rolled back years of memories. The familiar fields and pastures below were warm reminders of his roots.

Although ostensibly Eddie had come home to see his sister, he was a local celebrity with many other people to visit in Plainfield. His old friend U.S.G. Blakely announced his brief August homecoming in his newspaper, the *Plainfield Enterprise.* Reporting the event five days after Eddie flew in, Blakely noted: "The shouts of the aviators could plainly be heard when the engine would stop, which it frequently did while the plane was making a dive and it of course was guessed by the populace that 'Skinny' was flying home. Sure enough the plane soon landed in the Gate's pasture where Gardner had alighted before and then all knew it was 'Skinny.'" No one would have guessed that this trip was to be Eddie's last visit home.

In May 1921, Eddie entered his Nebraska Aircraft Corporation plane in the individual aerobatics competition at the Holdrege, Nebraska, aviation tournament. The tangible prize was a loving cup, but more than any trophy, Eddie wanted the glory of being the best flier to complete the required 30-minute aerial display.

By now he had been with the Nebraska company for 18 months. That was a long time for Eddie. He knew his routine by heart. He wasn't the least bit nervous before crowds. On the contrary, his employer praised his good judgment and expertise, saying that he was always "a skillful and careful pilot."

While Eddie was determined to be a show stopper for the crowd of about 10,000, his performance at the Holdrege tournament was somewhat lackluster. In the opinion of the three-member panel of judges, nearly all of his moves were flawed.

He left the ground at 4:22 p.m. and began with three wingovers, which the judges rated as "good"; followed by eight revolution spins, which got an equally mediocre rating; and three "perfect" loops. Next he performed two wingovers, which weren't up to par, followed by a "good" falling leaf, and six "perfect" loops.

He concluded his performance with a fairly good Immelman turn; another falling leaf, which wasn't any better than the last one; and a tailspin as a finale. This was one stunt too many.

"We were watching him very closely until he was within 50 feet of the ground, he had not reversed his controls, showing that he did not realize that he was too close to the earth," said P.H. Green, one of the three judges.

"When an aviator makes a long tailspin like that, the earth seems to be going one way and the plane another, so that it is a very jumbled up picture and it is exceedingly difficult to determine distance," Green told reporters covering the show.

Eddie may have miscalculated the amount of maneuvering room

he had available, as Green theorized, or there may have been another reason for the crash, as Lipsner wanted to believe. In his memoirs, the ever loyal Lipsner grasped for something other than pilot error to explain Eddie's fatal accident. Perhaps he sought to save face for his long fallen friend, keeping the memory of Eddie's accomplishments from being tarnished.

Lipsner attributed the accident to the goggles his friend was wearing at the time. They weren't Eddie's, Lipsner insisted. He had borrowed them from another flier and they didn't fit well. Lipsner reasoned that they must have somehow affected the veteran airman's vision, if only for a split second, but just long enough at a crucial moment to cause him to hit the ground. But Lipsner wasn't there. He wasn't a witness and all he could do was speculate.

Ira Biffle was on hand, however. He had come to the show with Eddie to work the crowd and had watched his colleague's performance the whole time.

"Gardner went into a tailspin at 1,200 feet and appeared at all times to have complete control of the ship," Biffle told newspaper reporters afterwards. At first he said that "It seemed to me that he tried to land [directly] from the spin, as he was just in a good position to make a landing."

Later Biffle remembered that there had been strong southeast winds blowing and theorized that perhaps the wind had caught the plane just as Eddie was about to right the ship, spinning the plane around uncontrollably and forcing him down too near to the ground to avoid impact.

It all happened so fast that Biffle wasn't certain what had gone wrong. One minute Eddie was flying just fine, a split second later he had harpooned his plane into the soft soil, burying the nose of the ship well up to the radiator.

Biffle ran to the crash site like a panicked animal running from a

Eddie reportedly was wearing these goggles when he crashed in Nebraska. This artifact, and other items belonging to Eddie, were donated to the National Postal Museum by Benjamin Lipsner.

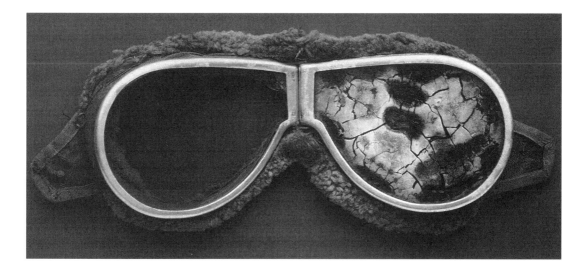

ferocious beast. His only thoughts were to aid his chum.

Curious spectators also swarmed the fallen plane, surrounding it to the point that it was nearly impossible to extract the injured pilot. Even after Eddie was pulled free from the wreckage the throng of onlookers left little room for the flier to be laid out on the dirt.

Biffle was quickly beside his comrade. Eddie's face looked terrible. His forehead appeared to have been crushed and his nose was obviously broken. Biffle also noticed other injuries. "The handle of the throttle was broken and Gardner's wrist was skinned," he sobbed, thinking back afterwards as he recounted details for reporters. "I believe that he held the lever to the last," he stated.

Neither Biffle nor anyone among the gawking crowd had any way of knowing what other injuries Eddie had sustained, but everyone knew that he needed serious medical help.

Remarkably, Eddie wasn't dead. The softness of the earth had apparently cushioned the impact enough to keep him from being killed outright. He was dazed but lucid enough to ask to see his plane. Gingerly, his rescuers lifted him up just far enough so that he could survey the wreckage. "The ship was alright," those on hand recalled him muttering.

In reality, neither the plane nor Eddie were in very good shape.

Eddie's next thoughts were to somehow get home to Plainfield and the care of his family. But Plainfield was far away, especially for anyone in his condition. Instead he was taken by car to the nearest doctor's office for immediate care.

The local doctor was certain that Eddie had fractured his skull, but he could not ascertain how extensive his internal injuries were. Eddie was conscious upon arrival and he could move his limbs, which gave the doctor hope; but country physicians have their limits and Eddie clearly needed greater care. Arrangements were made to transport him by train to the hospital at Lincoln.

The Plainfield boy had wanted to give the crowd at Holdrege a show-stopping performance, and sadly he had. Shocked spectators began leaving the show grounds almost immediately after the crash. In less than an hour the field was all but deserted. Few stayed to witness the remaining flights.

Eddie slipped into a coma shortly before his train arrived in Lincoln at 11:55 p.m. He was immediately taken to St. Elizabeth's Hospital. Around midnight he came out his coma briefly enough to ask his attendant where he was. Then he slipped back into an unconsciousness from which he never recovered.

Mercifully, Eddie Gardner died at about 3 o'clock on the morning of May 6, 1921. He died the way he lived: quickly and alone.

Now "Turk Bird" would come home for keeps.

Eddie's mother and sister were notified of his death on Friday, May 6. His brother-in-law, George Spangler, immediately set about

arranging for the funeral and the movement of the body. The pilot's coffin arrived at the W.C. Wunderlich funeral parlor on Case Street on Saturday.

The Gardner plot in the Plainfield Cemetary contains the remains of Eddie, his father, and his mother.

The funeral ceremony was conducted in Eddie's sister's house. This was more fitting than having it in the local Methodist church, as Eddie hadn't been very religious.

Local folks turned out en mass to pay their respects. Floral offerings were everywhere, and Eddie was accorded military honors, even though he never really served in the strict sense. The fact that he was a civilian flying instructor with the Army during World War I was more than enough to qualify him for veterans status in the eyes of the people of Plainfield. Members of the Plainfield chapter of the War Mothers and the American Legion all showed up to honor Eddie.

His coffin was escorted to the cemetery by six ex-servicemen and childhood friends: Ed Countryman, Lester Shaw, Everett Wright, Robert Bill, Arthur Norton, and Milton Sonntag. Frank Tower, who had accompanied Eddie on his final visit to Plainfield the previous summer, returned to be with Eddie for one last time. As a tribute to the aviator, Tower circled above in his biplane as the funeral cortege left his sister's house for the Plainfield cemetery.

Also accompanying the funeral procession was the entire student body of the town's high school. Classes were dismissed so that the youngsters could pay their respects to the uncle of one of their classmates, Evelyn Spangler, and to a man who had given nearly all of them free rides in his plane at one time or another during his countless visits home.

Orva Pratt, considered the songbird of Plainfield, sang at the Spangler home and again at the grave site.

Eddie was laid to rest alongside his father in a family plot that was purchased in 1915 by his mother when Martin Gardner died. Although the plot was large enough to accommodate five, only three people were interred in the family plot: Martin in 1915, Eddie in 1921, and Mary Gardner Schaaf in 1925. Nellie Spangler, who died in 1967, was buried next to her husband, who predeceased her by a year, and was laid to rest in another section of the Plainfield Cemetery. Resting beside Nellie and George Spangler is their infant daughter, Pearlie, who died in 1901.

Eddie was home.

EPILOGUE

The Air Mail Service that Eddie Gardner helped inaugurate in 1918 would go through many changes in the coming years, changes that resulted from steadily advancing technology and the growing needs of a nation destined to become a world super-power. The organization would never be the same as the tight band of comrades that Benjamin Lipsner brought together, though the path that Eddie first blazed would be followed by many more air mail pilots, including Lindbergh and Amelia Earhardt, who would experience their own heights of fame and misfortune.

With the end of World War I, *Scientific American* advanced the notion "that the Government should consider very seriously having the Post Office Department employ the War Department to carry its aerial mail." This idea was considered an inexpensive way to train military pilots. Instead of having two appropriations, one for military aviation and one for the Air Mail Service, only one appropriation would be necessary. According to the February 8, 1919, *Scientific American* article, "where training was possible under actual commercial conditions, in which schedules must be maintained and discipline kept at its highest point, our military aviators would be more interested in their work than they would be in the relatively aimless flying at training schools."

This idea came on the heels of the successful transcontinental flight of four Army airplanes at Hazelhurst Field, Long Island, on January 7, 1921, and the start of the return journey to San Diego, California, a few days later.

Others, including visionaries such as Brigadier General Billy Mitchell, also saw the Air Mail Service as an ideal testing ground for the military. Writing in the December 1920 issue of *The American Review of Reviews,* he observed: "The United States Army has assisted the Post Office Department in every way possible to carry out its excellent work, fully realizing that in the development of an efficient Air Mail Service, not only will the greater incentive be given to civil aviation, but that all of that has a direct bearing on national defense, because all the crews, equipment, and particularly the airdromes, and airways, may be utilized by all our aviation in war and in going from one coast to the other."

Mitchell went one step further by proposing that the Army resume flying the mail. His rationale was that flying was a skill that must be constantly practiced to keep pilots in trim and, if the Army's appropriation was insufficient to furnish an effective Army Air Corps, perhaps then the best way to achieve the same result was to let the Army fly the mail. Others liked the idea. The *Pittsburgh Post* declared: "Aviation has long since passed the stage where it was an experiment, it has become more, too, than an invaluable military weapon." The Air Mail Service was an accepted part of America's postal system, despite the claims of some that it was a costly flash in the pan.

But others weren't so sure that either government agency needed to fly the mail. Some in Congress thought it was an expensive gimmick. On this score, many newspapers rushed to defend the Air Mail Service, including the *Omaha Bee,* which stated: "The same objections now being brought out against the Air Mail Service were once used in argument against Rural Free Delivery, the Postal Savings bank, and the parcel post."

Everyone associated with the Air Mail Service knew how vulnerable it was politically. Each year the same group of cantankerous congressmen fought to kill the air mail appropriations, complaining that it was too expensive and cost too many lives. A political cartoon in the *Sacramento Bee* underscored the human cost with a sketch of a blood-soaked letter addressed to Uncle Sam with the notation: "8 Airmail Pilots Killed ... Is It Worth the Price?"

Writing in *The American Review of Reviews,* Burt M. McConnell observed that, despite the death rate — which by 1927 amounted to one fatality per million miles flown — "the Air Mail Service, by its pioneering work, has advanced civil aviation in this country by at least ten years." In fact, compared to European airlines, which were heavily subsidized, the United States postal system carried more mail by air than all other nations.

America's air mail superiority was acknowledged around the world. When the British railway dispute in September 1919 halted much of the United Kingdom's mail delivery, some letters were carried by plane. But the British air mail service apparently had some shortcomings. Writing in *The Sunday London Times,* Major W.T. Blake stated "the Service was a rank failure, and the reason for this was obvious ... In America they do things differently, and in respect of the aerial-mail services have certainly given a lead to the world."

And the cost to run the service was not as steep as some in Congress claimed. *Current Opinion* magazine praised the service for its speed and economy, citing it for its "mounting importance." It also reported that "during the first three years of Air Mail Service the cost of flying averaged 85 cents per mile." By July 1921, costs would drop to 75 cents per mile.

Unbeknownst to those debating its merits back in the 1920s, air mail service would not only survive but would create the seed for today's modern commercial airline industry. Many of today's well-known commercial carriers were initially formed to compete for lucrative air mail contracts. An example of this was Transcontinental Air Transport and Western Air Express. Initially separate companies, they merged to form TWA at the postal service's insistance.

From Eddie Gardner and Max Miller to Chuck Yeager and Neil Armstrong, from Jennies and jets to rockets and the space shuttle, there is a clear, unbroken path. While that path is strewn with the wreckage of great men and women, it is also paved with their courage and determination. It calls to farm town boys and girls and city kids alike whenever they marvel at a letter received from a distant place and look to the skies. Eddie Gardner flew that piece of mail to them.

Photo Credits

Cover, National Postal Museum, Smithsonian Institution.

Page 4, Ione and Norman Mueller, Plainfield, Illinois.

Page 5, Ione and Norman Mueller, Plainfield, Illinois.

Page 7, Ione and Norman Mueller, Plainfield, Illinois.

Page 10, (Top) National Postal Museum, Smithsonian Institution.

Page 10, (Bottom) National Postal Museum, Smithsonian Institution.

Page 11, National Postal Museum, Smithsonian Institution.

Page 12, National Postal Museum, Smithsonian Institution.

Page 13, Beverly Hyde, Warrenton, Virginia.

Page 15, National Postal Museum, Smithsonian Institution.

Page 16, National Postal Museum, Smithsonian Institution.

Page 17, National Postal Museum, Smithsonian Institution.

Page 19, National Postal Museum, Smithsonian Institution.

Page 24, Smithsonian Institution Libraries.

Page 25, National Postal Museum, Smithsonian Institution.

Page 27, National Postal Museum, Smithsonian Institution.

Page 32, National Postal Museum, Smithsonian Institution.

Page 33, Smithsonian Institution Libraries.

Page 35, Kevin Allen, Smithsonian Institution.

Page 37, National Postal Museum, Smithsonian Institution.

Page 39, National Postal Museum, Smithsonian Institution.

Page 43, Kevin Allen, Smithsonian Institution.

Page 46, Smithsonian Institution Libraries.

Page 53, National Postal Museum, Smithsonian Institution.

Page 57, Smithsonian Institution Libraries.

Page 59, Smithsonian Institution Libraries.

Page 65 National Postal Museum, Smithsonian Institution.

Page 66, National Postal Museum, Smithsonian Institution.

Page 74, National Postal Museum, Smithsonian Institution.

Page 76, National Postal Museum, Smithsonian Institution.

Page 78, National Postal Museum, Smithsonian Institution.

Page 79, National Postal Museum, Smithsonian Institution.

Page 82, Smithsonian Institution Libraries.

Page 85, Jeff Tinsley, Smithsonian Institution.

Page 88, National Postal Museum, Smithsonian Institution.

Page 89, Jeff Tinsley, Smithsonian Institution.

Page 90, Smithsonian Institution Libraries.

Page 95, Jeff Tinsley, Smithsonian Institution.

Page 97, Elizabeth Little.

Back Cover, National Postal Museum, Smithsonian Institution.